TRIANGULAR ROAD

TRIANGULAR ROAD

a memoir

PAULE MARSHALL

BASIC
CIVITAS
BOOKS

A Member of the Perseus Books Group
New York

Books published by BasicCivitas are available at special discounts for bulk
purchases in the United States by corporations, institutions, and other organizations. For more information, please contact the Special Markets
Department at the Perseus Books Group, 2300 Chestnut Street, Suite
200, Philadelphia, PA 19103, or call (800) 810-4145, ext. 5000, or e-mail
special.markets@perseusbooks.com.

DESIGNED BY JEFF WILLIAMS

Library of Congress Cataloging-in-Publication Data

Marshall, Paule, 1929–
    Triangular road : a memoir / Paule Marshall.
       p. cm.
    ISBN 978-0-465-01359-3 (alk. paper)
    1. Marshall, Paule, 1929– 2. African American authors—
Biography. 3. Women and literature—United States—History—
20th century. 4. Hughes, Langston, 1902–1967. 5. African
Americans—Intellectual life—20th century. I. Title.

PS3563.A7223Z46 2008
813'.54—dc22

                                                    2008036671

10 9 8 7 6 5 4 3 2 1

AUTHOR'S NOTE

This book is an adaptation of a lecture series delivered at Harvard University in 2005 on the theme of "Bodies of Water"—specific rivers, seas and oceans—and their profound impact on black history and culture throughout the Americas.

CONTENTS

HOMAGE TO
MR. HUGHES

New York. Early May, 1965. The return address on the official-looking letter I retrieved from my mailbox read "United States Department of State, 301 Fourth Street, SW, Washington, D.C. 20547." Frankly, I registered only the words "department" and "state," "State Department," and instantly panicked, anticipating the worst. The letter just had to be bad news of some sort. Why else would the State Department be writing me? Was I perhaps being summoned to appear before a new Joe McCarthy–type subcommittee on Un-American Activities? It was the height of the Civil Rights Movement, after all, and my involvement in the northern front of the Struggle had to be known. The thing in my hand might well mean trouble.

When I finally managed to calm down enough to open the letter, its contents proved to be a different matter altogether. Rather than a dire summons, it turned out to be a once-in-a-lifetime plum of an invitation.

According to the letter, the world-renowned poet Langston Hughes would soon be conducting a month-long cultural tour of Europe for the government, during which he would be giving a series of readings as well as talks on African American literature. This was something Mr. Hughes had done for the State Department on a number of occasions in other parts of the world. Only this time he had insisted that two young writers, of his choosing, be included on the tour. And he had named me as one of the writers he wished to take with him.

The invitation in hand, I stood dumbstruck for the longest time. Langston Hughes! None other than the poet laureate of black America had chosen me to accompany him on a cultural tour of

Europe! Me, a mere fledgling of a writer, with only one novel and a collection of stories published to date! Why would someone of his stature so much as consider a novice like myself?

Perhaps I should not have been all that surprised. Mr. Hughes was known for the support and encouragement he extended to the generation of younger writers like myself who began publishing in the 1950s and early 1960s. The poet Gwendolyn Brooks, the playwright Lorraine Hansberry, Alice Walker, among others, have written of their indebtedness to him. In my case, he had been kind enough to attend the book party that launched my first novel, published in 1959, a somewhat standard coming-of-age tale about a girl not unlike myself born and raised in a Brooklyn community that was both African American and West Indian. The book party, held in a Harlem storefront, was just getting underway when, to the awe of everyone there, the great man appeared in the doorway. Mr. Hughes was in his early sixties by then. The handsome, soulful-looking young poet of the 1920s Harlem Renaissance had long been replaced by a somewhat paunchy, rapidly aging yet nonetheless urbane man of letters, every wave of his naturally wavy hair in place, and his trademark cigarette a permanent fixture between his lips.

There he stood, the poet who had long been a literary icon, come to celebrate with me, come to congratulate me on the favorable reviews my novel had received, there to beam at me like a paterfamilias whose offspring had done him proud.

To add to the celebration, I was eight months pregnant at the time. A book and a baby in the same year and produced within a month of each other! A feat I was never to manage again. Mr. Hughes also promptly congratulated me as well as my husband standing beside me on the upcoming baby.

Two years later, 1961, saw yet another instance of his thoughtfulness and support upon the publication of my second book, the collection of stories I mentioned earlier entitled *Soul Clap Hands and Sing*. A postcard arrived from Mr. Hughes, written in his distinctive green ink. "'Clap Hands' is about the prettiest looking book I ever saw," the card read. "It just now came. I look forward to reading it." His large boyish flourish of a signature at the bottom.

Then, when the collection won a modest award from the American Academy of Arts and Letters, who was the first person at the awards ceremony to come hurrying over to plant a congratulatory kiss, *à la française,* on either side of my face? None other than Mr. Hughes. Indeed, he might well have been instrumental in my receiving the award—perhaps recommending the collection to those he knew on the academy's selection committee.

The People's Poet continued to keep the novice in mind.

Now he had gone so far as to invite her to travel with him to Europe.

Would you perhaps be interested in accompanying Mr. Hughes on the tour? the State Department letter read. A dumb question if ever there was! It then went on to say that if, indeed, I was interested in participating in the tour, I would be required to come to Washington to be briefed beforehand. Anyone traveling overseas under the auspices of the United States Department of State first had to be briefed.

Feeling panicked again, I nonetheless took the plane to Washington.

A convicted felon in a Flannery O'Connor story I often teach says of the legal authorities that have finally succeeded in tracking him down: "They had the papers on me." Irrefutable evidence, that is, of his many crimes. Such, also, was my case, I discovered. The authorities in Washington "had the papers on me." They were compiled, "those papers," the incriminating evidence, inside a sizable accordion-style folder or dossier, *my dossier,* that confronted me on the desk in the State Department office where the briefing was being held.

From the size of the thing it had to contain a detailed account of my involvement in every political organization to which I had ever belonged, from the Communist Party fringe AYD (American Youth for Democracy), whose cause I had briefly embraced at age seventeen, to the Association of Artists for Freedom and Concerned Mothers for Justice, the two organizations within the northern front of the Movement in which I was most involved at present. The principal activity of the two organizations was fund-raising to support the voting rights efforts underway in the Deep South. The extensive file must also have included the transcript of every speech in which I had roundly taken the government to task. Also on record had to be a list of each rally, protest meeting, demonstration and march I had participated in, including the first-ever joint Civil Rights– Anti-Vietnam War march, which had taken place that past winter in Times Square. As usual, the FBI agents in their London Fog trench coats had been on hand, openly writing down names and taking photographs from the sidelines.

More material for the dossiers in Washington.

Marching alongside me, I recall, had been "a brother" who kept up a volatile whisper of "Burn, baby, burn / burn, baby, burn," the newest anthem at the time of a frustrated and enraged black urban America. (My childhood world of Bed-Stuy Brooklyn had rioted the previous year, entire blocks going up in flames.) The brother, his face half-buried in his turned-up coat collar, had brought to mind Jesse B. Semple, the highly popular Harlem Everyman and barroom philosopher that Mr. Hughes had created as a newspaper series in the 1940s. An angry Jesse B. Semple might have taken Duke Ellington's *A train* down from Harlem to mutter his incendiary mantra in the heart of Times Square. Had he actually existed there would have been a file in Washington on him also.

The government officer conducting the briefing turned out to be a rather matronly looking woman with graying blond hair, blue-gray eyes and the carefully cultivated neutral manner of a civil servant long on the job. Framed on either side of her desk by LBJ's official portrait and the flag on its eagle-crowned standard, she began our session by placing a hand lightly on my dossier. "Seems you've been fairly active." Said with an undefined half-smile as she slid the folder aside and began the briefing.

The woman first gave a capsule history of the government's cultural programs around the world, then went on to describe at some length our particular tour: the various European cities we would be visiting and the general nature of our activities. The United States Information Service (USIS) people in charge of "operations on the ground" in each city would have a detailed schedule of those activities. Later, on a lighter, more conversational note, she offered chatty little tidbits about some of the places we would be visiting: the white nights in Copenhagen could be somewhat disorienting; complaints about the food in London were largely justified; unfortunately, the month of May in Paris usually meant rain, off-and-on rain—although the city remained beautiful nonetheless. In fact, Paris was to be our base, she said. The tour would begin there, and we would regularly return to the City of Light following visits to other places on the itinerary.

The woman talked for close to an hour, yet, strangely, she never again mentioned the dossier, filled with my denunciations and actions against the government, lying between us on her desk.

She never again so much as glanced in its direction. So that while sitting there hearing her out, I found myself thinking of Joseph K., Franz Kafka's poor beleaguered hero of his classic novel, *The Trial.* With Joseph K., there had been "no papers on him," no file or folder, no record of a single word or action on his part against the state. Yet, in the novel, he is hounded and persecuted unto death by a faceless, all-powerful state.

Whereas my situation was the exact opposite. While my quarrel with the U.S. government was a matter of record—viz., the dossier—said government was apparently perfectly willing to treat me to an almost month-long, all-expense-paid trip to Europe, with *Paris* as the base! Surely Washington knew that I would be as outspoken abroad as at home. Why, then, agree to me accompanying Mr. Hughes? I sat puzzling over this as the briefing continued, only to conclude that the government might actually benefit by sending "an emissary" such as myself overseas. The fact that I would be openly critical of its policies could well serve as proof that the country was truly a democracy committed to respecting the First Amendment rights of even its most vocal detractors. Thus, Washington might well come out the winner every time I opened my mouth.

The longtime civil servant across the desk obviously understood this. Her somewhat flippant comment on my dossier: "Seems you've been fairly active." The way she had then relegated it to one side implied as much. The file might have been trotted out simply to put me on notice that Big Brother was watching and would continue to watch. So be it, then. The briefing over, I left Washington sans illusions. I would definitely go on the tour—this once-in-a-lifetime chance to travel with a world-famous writer; and I would speak my mind about said government when asked, even though my freedom to criticize might, ironically, redound to Washington's good. No matter. Speaking out would be a way of making use of being used—if, indeed, such was the case.

The tour was due to get underway shortly, so that once back in New York I quickly set about preparing to leave: first, making arrangements for the care of my young son, the book-party baby, and then putting aside the novel—my second—that I had been working on for some time. I also made sure to take along my one and only novel that Mr. Hughes had helped launch. Perhaps I might find a European publisher for it. Then, on the appointed day, still dazed by my good fortune, I took a taxi to Kennedy Airport along with William Melvin Kelley, the other writer Mr. Hughes had chosen.

Bill Kelley was another fledgling. A Harvard dropout who had abandoned his law studies for creative writing, he had also, like myself, so far published a novel and a collection of stories, both well reviewed. His novel, called *A Different Drummer,* was a highly experimental, mythic tale about a massive revolt in a southern town. Fed up with racism and a lifetime picking cotton, the entire black population suddenly picks up one day and abandons the place. They stage a biblical-style exodus, as it were, but not before they pour salt, tons of salt, over every cotton field in sight.

Mr. Hughes had promoted Bill Kelley's work as well, and had even hired him as a research assistant when he left Harvard to write full time.

Our benefactor, cigarette in place, stood waiting for us inside the terminal, a suitcase and a small satchel at his side. (The satchel I later learned held copies of his most recent books of poetry, which he intended to sell during the tour. Mr. Hughes was every bit a wandering bard in the old tradition, but a bard who also believed in the modern concept of TCB, i.e., taking care of the business of selling his books whenever and wherever possible.)

I had not seen him since the awards ceremony at the American Academy of Arts and Letters four years earlier, and he appeared noticeably older, his aging like the merciless hand of a giant steadily, relentlessly bearing down on him. The pressure of that hand, however, the weight of it, in no way diminished the cheery, paternal smile with which he greeted us, nor the aura and authority of his long reign as poet laureate. I can't speak for Bill Kelley, but I felt like bowing before his royal presence that day in the airport.

Rain. I awoke the Sunday morning following our arrival in Paris to an off-and-on spring rain outside my hotel room window. The State Department woman had been right after all. In a building across the way—which I later learned was the Moroccan student hostel; the Sorbonne was nearby—a bored-looking young woman cracked open a casement window, flipped out her cigarette and disappeared back inside. On the rain-soaked sidewalk below, an exasperated French papa stood struggling with both his windblown umbrella and his small son who was having a full-blown tantrum at his side, the child's screams desecrating the Sunday morning quiet.

A wet, noisy and inauspicious introduction to the City of Light. But no matter. It was nonetheless Paris, and I had at last set foot on its famous streets.

We were staying in the equally famous Latin Quarter, at a hotel named, oddly enough, the California. As hotels go, the California could not have qualified for even a one-star rating. (It has since been renovated and upgraded.) At the time, its small, plain rooms offered little aside from a bed, and its cramped lobby was made to double as a breakfast room: coffee and a single croissant each morning. Worse was the cubicle of an elevator. This was usually *en panne*—that is, out of order, not running. I'm sure that the State Department people on the ground in Paris would have gladly arranged far better accommodations for us. Mr. Hughes, though, had probably insisted on the California. The humble little *pension* was where he always stayed when in the city he considered his second home after Harlem.

The first Paris phase of the tour quickly became a busy round of lectures, readings, seminars, panels, panel discussions, colloquia, roundtables, roundtable discussions—and talks. Invariably, each of these was followed by a reception and more talk at the end of an already long day. The principal venues for most events were the Sorbonne and the American Cultural Center on Rue du Dragon, which was also the headquarters for the State Department people in charge of our tour. In addition, a large two-day seminar was held at Royaumont, a centuries-old abbey outside of Paris that had been converted into a conference center. Our first evening there, the three of us read from our work in the great resounding stone nave of the abbey's ancient sanctuary.

While the stated subject of the events was African American literature, the Q&A sessions that followed the formal presentations were invariably less about literature and more about the Freedom Struggle underway in the States. The progressive-minded young graduate students and scholars who largely made up our audience were eager for first-hand information on the Movement and the government's response to the mounting pressure for change.

Although he was the star attraction, Mr. Hughes, for whatever reason, tended to leave such discussions to Bill Kelley and myself, the young Turks, as it were. And we were only too willing to stand in for him. In the most graphic terms possible we described the violence meted out to innocent protesters in the Deep South—the police dogs being sicced on them, the policemen's billyclubs beating them to the ground, the huge fire-engine water hoses turned on them full blast, and black children as young as twelve being thrown in jail. We also pointed out that the principal issue at the moment in the Civil Rights Movement was the passage of a comprehensive voting rights bill. All efforts were focused on pressuring Congress to pass such a bill this very year in spite of the fierce opposition of the southern members in both houses and what was seen as stalling on the president's part. At a recent meeting of the Association of Artists for Freedom held at Town Hall in New York, I had been among those, including James Baldwin, Ruby Dee, Ossie Davis, Lorraine Hansberry and others, denouncing LBJ for his inaction on the bill.

Racism. Black/white relations. Our audiences repeatedly brought up the subject. Again, Bill Kelley and I didn't hesitate, but spoke in detail about the deep and lingering racist nature of American society, citing the political, social and economic institutions and policies—including government policies—that sustained and perpetuated the problem.

Again, for the most part, Mr. Hughes usually maintained a reflective silence. He might have been remembering his own personal trials and tribulations at the hands of the U.S. government. Wasn't he the poet, after all, whom said government had once labeled "perhaps the most dangerous radical in America"? The poet whom it had hauled before McCarthy's infamous subcommittee in the early fifties? Where to save his career, the poet, it's said, had disavowed his socialist and communist principles? For this he had been severely criticized, even denounced by many in the black community: He had betrayed W. E. B. Du Bois; he had betrayed Paul Robeson—those two giants who had remained faithful to the cause.

All this the poet had endured only to find himself once again embraced by black America as well as called upon by the government to serve as a cultural ambassador around the world. The contradiction and irony, the illogic of it all perhaps accounted for the expression that read "white folks, black folks, there's no understanding them" that came over his face at times.

Among my mementos of the tour is a photograph in *Paris Match* of Mr. Hughes and myself at a lecture toward the end of our initial stay in Paris. (By then Bill Kelley was no longer with us. Early in the tour, he received word from the States of an adjunct teaching job, and as a recently married man with a baby on the way, he immediately flew home. It would be just Mr. Hughes and me from then on.) In the *Paris Match* photograph I can be seen inveighing as

PAS EN TEMPS MAIS EN LIEU

C'est sous un titre ambigu et difficile à traduire, « The Chosen Place, The Timeless People », que Paule Marshall publie son nouveau roman. Considérée comme l'une des romancières noires les plus douées, très avertie de la condition des habitants des « Indes occidentales », notamment les Barbades, elle a situé l'action dans ce décor exotique qu'elle aime et où elle a vécu — encore qu'elle soit née à Brooklyn.

Les principaux personnages du livre sont cependant des Blancs ; il s'agit d'un trio de spécialistes du Tiers Monde, apparemment dévoués à la cause du développement économique, et dont l'attitude, sur le terrain,

Paule Marshall discute avec Langston Hughes lors d'une visite au Centre du Dragon.

révélera l'étroitesse d'esprit, le racisme ou l'inefficacité. En face d'eux, se dresse la figure d'une meneuse de jeu noire — sorcière, sainte et révolutionnaire — dont l'auteur a tracé un portrait vigoureux. Paule Marshall confirme dans ce livre les qualités qui avaient fait le succès de ses deux premiers romans, « Brown Girl Brownstones » et « Soul Clap Hands and Sing ».

A signaler aussi la réimpression d'une anthologie classique et introuvable de la littérature noire, « The Negro Caravan », dont la première édition, en 1941, était passée inaperçue et qui est devenue par la suite une institution nationale. D'aucuns regrettent toutefois qu'un ouvrage de ce genre soit mis en vente au prix exorbitant de 35 dollars.

JOHN O'HARA

UNE PROVIDENCE PARTICULIERE

Avec « A Special Providence », Richard Yates, l'auteur d'inoubliables « Histoires de Solitude », n'ajoute rien à sa gloire. L'ouvrage raconte l'émancipation d'un jeune homme, échappé des jupons de sa mère.

Mais une Providence veille sur John O'Hara, l'auteur du « Rendez-vous à Samarcande » (ville de l'Uzbekistan dont le traducteur français conservait curieusement le nom américain « Samarra »). Après une trentaine d'ouvrages fort discutés dont, selon les critiques, un seul (« From the Terrace », sinon « Ten North Frederick »), justifie sa réputation, John O'Hara, si souvent tenu pour déchu, trouve encore le moyen de déclencher des polémiques avec son dernier livre, « Lovey Childs » — une

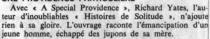

Discussion at Centre du Dragon reported in *Paris Match*.

usual against Washington, while Mr. Hughes sits silent nearby, his aging face propped on his fist, his cigarette pasted to his lips, and what might well have been his own considerable outrage and anger kept carefully under wraps. *The Weary Blues,* published 1922. In the *Paris Match* photo Mr. Hughes seems to epitomize the title of his very first published book of poems.

Not that the poet didn't give way to anger at times. This occurred at Africa House in London, the second city on our itinerary. The lecture at Africa House followed the pattern established in Paris, in that our talk on African American literature was largely supplanted by a discussion of the Movement. Only this time the discussion took an ugly turn as a number of the young British-born blacks in the audience began personally attacking Mr. Hughes. They ignored me—I was an unknown after all—and leveled their criticism at him alone. Essentially they accused him of a lack of militancy. Why wasn't he to be seen in the front line of the marches taking place in the South? Why wasn't he speaking out in the same manner as Amiri Baraka, James Baldwin, Stokely Carmichael et al.? Seems that he was as conservative and as much of an accommodationist as Roy Wilkens, Ralph Ellison and their ilk. . . .

The Weary Blues look on the poet's face again. It lasted only briefly, though, this time. Instead, seated beside me at our table on stage, Mr. Hughes put aside his cigarette, drew the microphone close, and for the first time there was an unmistakable edge of outrage in his voice as he began speaking. Going on at some length, he informed his young critics that the revolution—Mr. Hughes used the word "revolution"—underway at present in black America had not begun yesterday nor would it end tomorrow. He and his generation had done their part: marching, demonstrating, picketing; they had protested the horrendous lynchings and burnings of the 1920s and '30s; had defended the innocent—the Scottsboro Boys, 1931. Nine young black men their age falsely accused of raping a white woman and railroaded for life. The fight to free them, in which he had been deeply involved, had gone on for years. All of this happening long before any of them in the audience had been born. . . .

Mr. Hughes subjected the young black Brits to a crash course in twentieth-century African American history.

There was monumental work still to be done, he concluded. So that rather than passing judgment or making comparisons, instead of taking a superficial view of people and events, it was for them to educate themselves and to understand the complexity of a Struggle that fundamentally involved people of color around the world.

A shamefaced silence in Africa House.

There was yet another problem on the tour that, while completely different from the confrontation at Africa House, increasingly annoyed and then finally angered Mr. Hughes. This had to do with our meals. My benefactor loved to eat and drink well, and to do so on a regular basis—meaning three meals a day, with each meal, especially dinner, to be eaten in a leisurely way over good wine and nonacademic, nonintellectual, nonpolitical conversation. He apparently had had his fill of those conversations over the years and had grown weary. However, the schedule in London, which also included a nonstop round of meetings and talks in the city as well as visits to Leeds and Manchester, kept us as busy as we had been in Paris. We often found ourselves eating dinner so late in the evening that we would be too exhausted and talked out to enjoy it. Mr. Hughes was not pleased. "Paul-e . . ." (He insisted on calling me Paul-e, although the "e" on my name is silent. But who was I to correct him?) "Paul-e, these State Department folks in Paris are messing with us. Here, they got us singing for our supper morning, noon and night only to come up short every time on the supper, the main meal of the day."

Matters came to a head one evening on a trip from London to Oxford, where Mr. Hughes had been invited to read by the university's Poetry Society. Earlier in the day, we had again been kept on the go without a proper meal, so that by the time we boarded the train to Oxford late that afternoon, a thoroughly exasperated Mr. Hughes, with me in tow, headed straight for the first-class dining car—hungry. We were going to treat ourselves, he declared, to a steak dinner and the best wine to be had on the train. To our dismay there was a long English queue outside the first-class dining car. Worse, by the time we were finally seated, then finally served, and had tucked into our steak dinners and wine, there came the announcement that Oxford was only minutes away. That did it. A still hungry and now thoroughly angry Mr. Hughes ordered the waiter to recork our bottle of wine, he instructed me to take charge of the food, and we alighted into the Oxford Poetry Society's distinguished welcoming committee with the wine hidden amid the books for sale in Mr. Hughes's satchel and with me carrying—as discreetly as possible—two doggie bags of half-eaten steaks.

Upon returning to our base in Paris for a second round of activities there, Mr. Hughes took the State Department people "on the ground" to task, and the schedule was changed to provide us with definite mealtimes as well as a few evenings to ourselves. Ever the guide and mentor, Mr. Hughes used those free evenings to introduce me—a little provincial from Brooklyn—to the city's fabled nightlife of bars, cabarets, *boîtes*, cafés, *caves* (underground jazz spots), nightclubs, *brasseries* and more bars. Mr. Hughes had his favorites and saw to it that I sampled any number of them in his company.

Also, a literary agent I had contacted during our initial stay in Paris had promising news on our return about a possible French edition of my novel.

More cause for celebration.

During our evenings on the town, my "tour guide" proved to be indefatigable. In fact, as soon as dusk fell, Mr. Hughes seemed to promptly slough off, like so much dead skin, *The Weary Blues* that overcame him at times during the day, and to metamorphose into "a man open to people and parties," as his fellow poet and Paris habitué, Ted Joans, once described him. A postcard Mr. Hughes sent me sometime after our time together in Europe ended attests to his party-going prowess. He was back in his second home again, this time to celebrate the opening in Paris of James Baldwin's play, *The Amen Corner.*

"Paris again," the card read. "Loved finding your letter on my return from a week in the Tunisian sun. Jimmy Baldwin threw a BIG spareribs party for the <u>Amen Corner</u> cast last night all night. (I were there). Fate and deadlines are catching up with me, so guess I better come home. Oh, Gawd! L. H."

Truth is, Mr. Hughes was Night People, that odd and perhaps lonely breed of humankind who are most vividly alive and at their best creatively during the hours between midnight and dawn. Aware that I was not of the breed and needed my sleep, most evenings my tour guide would faithfully escort me back to the Hotel California at a reasonable hour. Ever the gentleman, he would see me safely up the unreliable elevator, after which the poet "open to people and parties" would then once again vanish into the Parisian night, not to reappear until morning and his breakfast of coffee and croissant in the California's lobby.

"Paris," he once wrote. "There you can be whatever you want to be. Totally yourself."

Copenhagen was next on the itinerary with another full schedule of readings and talks. Copenhagen was no gay Paree. After the City of Light, the Danish capital appeared somber and stone-gray, a heavily medieval architectural gray. What distinguished it, of course, were its white nights, the sky above the city remaining the clear translucent blue of a freshwater lake from sunset until sunrise and then all through the day.

Mr. Hughes took advantage of those pale-blue Scandinavian nights to indulge another of his pastimes: reminiscing, reliving his youth. Once the official day was over and we had had our leisurely dinner with wine, part of the night was then spent in his suite at the hotel, with Mr. Hughes, a brilliant raconteur, re-creating for me the glory days of the Harlem Renaissance: the writers, musicians, painters, philosophers et al. who were among his circle of friends; the small magazines in which he first started to publish—one called *Fire* that lasted all of one issue, and *The Crisis*, the magazine of the NAACP, which is still in existence today. He told riotous stories about the Harlem literati and "niggerati" (those pretentious black folk who loved to put on the dog). "The poet open to people and parties" described for me the rent parties he attended during the Great Depression. (A quarter or fifty cents at the door helped your host pay the rent.)

Moreover, Mr. Hughes clarified for me the ideological war during that period between the politically radical but aristocratic W. E. B. Du Bois and the flamboyant populist Marcus Garvey—with Du Bois calling for the creation of a "Talented Tenth" of intellectuals to lead the struggle for full citizenship, and Garvey placing the working class, the masses in the vanguard. "Rise up, you mighty race!" he exhorted them.

My benefactor often spent the better part of the night educating the fledgling about a period of our history that had been all but omitted in the standard textbooks of my day.

Then there were the stories from his travels around the world. The poet had been "a travelin' man" ever since he dropped out of Columbia University at age nineteen and signed on as a mess boy on a freighter bound for Africa. And, yes, he did actually throw his textbooks overboard as he set sail.

The Big Sea.

I Wonder as I Wander.

Those were his two travel memoirs. I had read *The Big Sea* as a teenager and had privately vowed, even back then, to follow the example of its author. Not only would I become a writer, but a travelin' woman as well.

During those Copenhagen nights, Mr. Hughes became a kind of West African griot, a tribal elder passing down black American culture and history in an endless wreath of cigarette smoke while nursing a shot glass of gin at his side, taken straight, no chaser.

Berlin, along with any number of other cities in Germany, was next on the itinerary; then it would be back to Paris again. I would not, though, be accompanying Mr. Hughes on this leg of the tour. It was time for me to return home. There was my son's increasingly unhappy six-year-old voice over the phone. (He was being taken care of by my sister.) There was, as well, the increasingly nagging thought of the novel I had put aside. Also, I had heard from friends that massive demonstrations were being planned to once again pressure Congress and the president to pass the voting rights bill before the year ended. I definitely wanted to be home for that also.

Mr. Hughes understood. His generation had done its part, as he had pointed out at Africa House in London. The ongoing Struggle was continuing with mine. *"La lutta continua!"* The poet understood as much and would complete the State Department tour on his own. Keeping to the schedule, he flew to Germany at dawn one morning, hours before my flight back to the States was due to depart. Ever thoughtful, ever the gentleman, Mr. Hughes left not one, but two parting gifts for me at the hotel's reception desk. The note that accompanied them, written in his large hand, in his signature green ink, on the hotel's stationery, is another precious memento.

He had not forgotten our aborted steak dinner on the train to Oxford.

I never had the opportunity to travel with Mr. Hughes again. He nonetheless continued to befriend me and to support my work. Along with the notes and postcards he sent from his travels, he also telephoned from time to time whenever he was in New York. My phone would ring around 11 P.M., and right away I'd know: Mr. Hughes, Night People. Ostensibly, he was calling simply to chat before settling down to work for the night. Actually, the calls had more to do with checking on my output for the day. "How did it go today, Paul-e?" (Still insisting on the feminizing "e" to my name.) "How many pages did you get done?" He was not pleased when all I might have to report for the day was a short paragraph or two that in all likelihood had ended up in the wastepaper basket after being revised to death. A highly prolific, seemingly effortless writer such as Mr. Hughes could not understand a slowpoke like myself who could spend hours laboring over a single sentence. Moreover, as someone who thoroughly enjoyed being famous, he was concerned about the effect of my snail's pace on my career. Publish or perish wasn't only true of the academy. The literary establishment could be equally cruel. My benefactor tried warning me in so many words of the obscurity I might be courting in taking so long to produce so little.

He once lost patience with me. "Paul-e," he cried over the phone. "Do you realize that I have a book out for every year that you've been alive?"(I was in my mid-thirties at the time.) "You better get busy."

He certainly kept busy. It's said—and this might well be apocryphal—that up to the moment of his death in the PolyClinic Hospital in New York he had been at work on a new poem. It must not have been going well, because with the last of his strength Mr. Hughes is supposed to have flung his writing pad and pencil across the room.

James Mercer Langston Hughes. Mr. Hughes. For me, he was a loving taskmaster, mentor, teacher, griot, literary sponsor and treasured elder friend. I miss him. Decades have passed since his death in 1967 and I still miss him. A poem of his speaks to that continuing sense of loss.

I loved my friend.
He went away from me.
There's nothing more to say.
The poem ends,
Soft as it began
I loved my friend.

I'VE KNOWN RIVERS:
THE JAMES RIVER

> . . . where the water falleth so rudely and with
> such violence, as not any boat can pass.
>
> —CAPTAIN JOHN SMITH, MAY 1607

Richmond, Virginia. Labor Day, 1998. It's a near ninety-degree September morning, summer still very much in force, but without the dog-day heat and humidity that descends like judgment on this capital city of 200,000 during July and August.

A friend and I have decided to spend part of the holiday on the north bank of the James River, close to where it flows through the heart of Richmond—or River City, as the Virginian capital is called due to the importance of the James in its creation. Spawned in the Allegheny Mountains to the west, *"the ri-vah,"* as the local folk call the James in an affectionate drawl, courses east some three hundred miles across the state until it reaches Jamestown, the museum of a town that was the first permanent English settlement in America. And after Jamestown, the Atlantic Ocean.

The James. It's America's most historic river.

This is the first time my friend and I have visited this particular stretch of the north bank. To reach the water, we find we will have to negotiate a riverbank that at first glance looks as high and steep and thickly forested as the side of a mountain. There's a crude pathway of log steps to help facilitate the descent. Yet even with the logs, I'm finding the going difficult. Not so my friend, whose name happens to be Virginia, in keeping with the part of her family history that is linked to the Old Dominion. An energetic octogenarian, Virginia is managing the treacherous climb down with all the aplomb of a seasoned outdoorsman. Small-built and sinewy, my friend seems blessed with a constitution that will permit her to reach the age of a hundred and beyond still fit in body, clear in mind and undaunted in spirit.

Taking heart from her confidence, I follow her down.

The old-growth forest of trees is so thick we can neither glimpse nor hear the river, and only intermittently make out the sky. Then, perhaps ten minutes into our descent, a pair of railroad tracks abruptly brings the log stairway to an end. This section of the riverbank had long been leveled and graded to accommodate yet another branch of the southland's vast CSX Railway System that had once had its hub in Richmond.

During its ascendancy the capital city had been both a river *and* a railroad town.

A raised and enclosed metal platform takes us safely over the CSX tracks to the lower portion of the riverbank. Here, there's no log pathway, only the narrowest of trails that seems to drop straight as a plumb line down through the trees and thick underbrush. We're willing to risk it, though, because now, suddenly, we hear the river. Slowly, Virginia in the lead, we inch our way down the trail until it finally, unceremoniously, deposits us on a hot, deserted little sandspit of a beach with the James River at its feet.

First thing is to find someplace to sit that's out of the sun. A quick search turns up a large, somewhat flat stone that calls to mind the oversized ottoman to an easy chair. Best of all, the ottoman stone is lodged near the water's edge under a tall, canopy-wide willow oak tree that with each breeze seems to transform itself into a huge East Indian punkah fan over our heads.

An ideal spot. And, it turns out, we will have it all to ourselves for the entire morning. The rest of Richmond has chosen to spend the holiday elsewhere.

Recovering from the climb down, we simply sit for a time quietly taking in the river—the rockbound river. This stretch of the James is a veritable minefield of boulder-size antediluvian rocks that might have been flung there millennia ago by the quick-to-anger God of the Old Testament.

Another one of his commandments might have been broken and, in a tantrum, he had rained down rocks instead of his usual fire. Indeed, the Old Fellow can still be heard fulminating those times when the James at floodtide comes roaring downstream in a whitewater chaos of uprooted trees, hurtling rocks, unmoored boats, drowned dogs, cats, cows and even the occasional human.

This morning the river is far from floodtide, and the two of us—ladies well beyond a certain age (I'm in my seventies)—sit taking our ease beside it.

Virginia and I have been friends since I came to live in Richmond over twenty years ago. Our immediate bond was discovering that in our younger days we had both been travelin' women, who had loved moving around the world. Virginia had lived abroad for years at a time. Her husband, a visual artist, had also been a cultural attaché in various U.S. embassies in the Middle East and Asia—one of few blacks to hold such posts. His tours of duty had seen them living in Egypt, Afghanistan and Sri Lanka for extended periods. All that had been decades ago, though, and my friend was now a widow and former teacher who had retired back to the state for which she had been named.

In my case, a job brought me to Richmond. I was offered a position as writer-in-residence at Virginia Commonwealth University (VCU), a large research university in the capital city. It was a two-year contract, another in a long list of such contracts. Like many a fiction writer, I largely supported my "habit" with temporary teaching stints here and there across the country. For one, two and sometimes three years I would teach graduate level courses on writing the short story and the novel. The emphasis in class discussions had largely to do with the craft and techniques employed in the two forms. The list of universities where I taught were legion, and included Yale, Columbia University, the Iowa Writers' Workshop, the University of California at Berkeley, as well as any number of far less prestigious institutions, such as the present Virginia Commonwealth University. Also, this would be my first time venturing below the Mason-Dixon Line. True, I knew that Virginia was not considered

"*South*" in the same way as Nina Simone's *Mississippi Goddamn;* nevertheless I had misgivings. I needed a job, though, at the time. Then, to my surprise, once I completed the two years of my contract at VCU, I was invited to stay on as a permanent member in the graduate creative-writing program. And it would be a tenured position. My first real job and tenured at that! The offer seemed almost predestined, as if it was somehow important that I remain for a time in the former capital of the Confederacy. In fact, I had already settled in during the two years of the contract: had found a modest apartment, started another novel and made a few friends, Virginia being the most simpatico.

We haven't seen each other in a while—I was away for most of the summer—so we start the Labor Day morning by catching up on the news. I tell her about the African American writers' conference in Paris in which I participated; then, afterward, staying on in the City of Light. She, in turn, fills me in on events in black Richmond during my absence. We also bring each other up to date on our respective children: Virginia's three and my one. Their middle-aged lives in scattered places. Books: She's presently reading a long novel set in India, a country she often visited while living in Sri Lanka. I tell her about a talented young woman writer from Haiti whose work I discovered while away.

The morning passing in leisurely talk. A perfect day unfolding. Soon, as if to underscore the perfection, there comes the sound of laughter from upriver. A rafting party. Off in the distance a flotilla of several large bright-blue rubber rafts can be seen performing a bouncy dance downstream toward us. The rafters, twenty-and-thirty-year-old somethings, all of them white, are making a noisy show of maneuvering their bulbous craft through the moderate whitewater and rocks.

They're marking the end of summer with an excursion down the James.

To avoid the dangerous currents midstream, they are keeping to the south bank where there's a safe channel. The rocks on that side also form several swimming holes, so that when the flotilla reaches them, a number of the rafters strip to their bathing suits and take to the water, splashing and frolicking like two-year-olds in a playground pool.

"I wonder if they realize how polluted this river is?" I say.

Having read up on it, I know that the once-pristine James has become over time a dumping ground not only for generations of human and animal waste but, worse, dangerous industrial contaminants as well: PCBs, PCTs, TBT (tributylin), nitrogen, ammonia, fecal coliform, Kepone, toxic mercury, creosote and pathogens of all kinds. Add also tons of sulfuric acid from the now-defunct Civil War arsenals, armories and munitions plants whose ruins still line the riverbank in downtown Richmond. Include as well the over six hundred chemicals associated with tobacco and Philip Morris, the state's prime industry.

"They're trying to clean it up, I hear," says Virginia, speaking of the river. "I still wouldn't go near it, though. But our young swimmers probably feel they're immune."

We raise our bottles of spring water in a toast to youth and its illusion of immunity.

The swim over, the excursionists clamber back aboard the rafts, strap on their life jackets and helmets, take up their paddles, and continue their rollicking ride downriver.

An odd sensation as I watch the flotilla disappear around the final bend that leads to the city: My mind slowly divides in two, half of it attending to the pleasant conversation my friend and I are having, while the other half quietly slips away to accompany the rafters on what's left of their trip.

They don't have much farther to go. The Labor Day junket will end once they reach the heart of downtown Richmond. There, due to what's said to be an ancient geological rift in the riverbed, the James profoundly changes character. Like my mind at the moment, it divides in two. The city's downtown marks "the Falls," meaning the end of the rock-bound James, "where the water falleth so rudely and with such a violence, as not any boat can pass," and the beginning of the river's long, smooth tidal basin that is navigable all the way to historic Jamestown and the Atlantic Ocean some sixty miles downstream.

Rough water and smooth. They lie side by side right below the city's skyscraper office and commercial buildings, banks and brokerage houses. Richmond is the only American city that has whitewater rapids moiling through its business center. Indeed, it was the combination of the whitewater power of the James fueling the new industries, together with the tidewater offering safe passage to the ships up from the Atlantic, with their chattel cargo, that made for the wealth and status the Old Dominion would enjoy for nearly two centuries.

By now the rafting party has reached the dividing line between rough water and smooth. The joyride down the Falls of the James is over. A bus will take the young twenty-thirty-somethings back to their starting point miles upriver, where, over a few beers, they will noisily recap the thrills of the morning.

Youth.

The excursion over, I should also head back to the north bank and my friend. Instead, the truant part of my mind continues along what is now the tidal James, even though it knows what it will encounter there: all those wrenching land-marks—and all of them within the city limits. They begin, those landmarks, with the replace-ment of the notorious old Mayo's Bridge that had been the first to link the river's north and south banks. The original had been nothing more than a crude wooden footbridge that often threatened, it was said, to give way under the weight of the chained and coffled nightly traffic it had been hastily built to accommodate.

Farther ahead: yet another landmark. This one the ruins of the extensive docks that once lined both sides of the James near Richmond, with the largest, busiest and best known of them all—the Big Daddy of them all—the Manchester Docks on the south bank.

The condition of the chattel cargo was such af-ter the long weeks, sometimes months, at sea, that to placate the townsfolk who complained about the sight and smell of the shipments, a decree was drawn up declaring that the chattel were to be brought into town only at night. Only then was it permitted to march them, chained together at the neck and legs, along the high, precipitous south riverbank over to the rattletrap Mayo's Bridge, which, in turn, deposited them in Olde Richmond Towne on the north bank, its sleep undisturbed. Then, at daybreak, in a place apart from the town proper called the Bottom, amid a cohort of traders, agents, suppliers, exporters, commodities brokers, auctioneers, and scores of independent buyers large and small, the shipment would be put up for sale.

Richmond, VA. It was the principal port of entry for Africans brought to the New World in the eighteenth century.

The trade was so brisk, the money to be made so plentiful, that often the buying and selling took place on board the ship the moment it docked, or even on the dock itself. Other times, "scrambles" were held in the small towns and villages along the tidal James before the ships reached Richmond. In a "scrambles," the chattel cargo was taken from the hold, off the boat, and herded into a fenced-in yard or pen or stockade with a locked gate. Waiting outside would be a crowd of eager buyers, each with a long rope. Then, once the gate was opened, the "scrambles" began, with the buyers dashing about the yard or pen or stockade, desperate to lasso and corral as many chattel as possible never mind their condition: the stench, the running sores, the caked shit. Desperate, the buyers often turned on each other. Many an ugly tug-of-war took place over a choice find in the shipment.

The demand was that great. The Old Dominion —which was brand new back then—needed an endless supply of John Henry muscle, brawn and sweat to produce what became the cash crop of all time. Tobacco. Yes: peanuts, cotton, hogs, and everything else having to do with the land, but above all, in Virginia, it was King Tobacco, "the jovial weed," to which all of Europe was addicted at the time.

Date: October 6, 1995

Place: Downstate Hospital, Brooklyn, New York

Patient's Name: Anita Burke Wharton

Time of Death: 3:16 a.m.

Cause of Death: Pulmonary Hypertension

Whenever my sister, an inveterate New Yorker, came to visit me in Richmond, she always brought along a large empty carry-on in addition to her suitcase. The carry-on was for the dozen or more cartons of Virginia Slims she intended to purchase during her stay.

This was Philip Morris country, after all, where her favorite brand was suddenly "a steal" compared to the price in New York. My sister had always been thrifty. Naturally, I was always glad to see her, yet dismayed by what might well have been the principal reason for her visits. And there was no reasoning or pleading with her. "Something's got to take you," would be her fatalistic comeback. With each visit, her breathing became more labored. When she could no longer physically make the trip, I was asked, then ordered (I was the kid sister) to purchase the cartons and mail them to her. She would send me a check for the amount. Each time I refused, and each time she slammed down the phone on me, furious that she would be forced to pay New York prices. Which she did until the end.

In addition to everything having to do with cultivating the land, the same muscle, brawn and sweat also figured in the rail system (CSX) that soon reached from Florida to Mississippi, with its hub Olde Richmond Towne. "Cutting cross ties is nasty work to do," declared Nate Shaw, grandson of chattel, in the story of his life recorded in a volume called *All God's Dangers*.

And what of the great neoclassical Jeffersonian state capital buildings in downtown Richmond that are second only to those in Washington? Chattel labor again.

They also worked as hired-out hands (their wages paid to their owners) in the factories, mills, tobacco warehouses and munitions plants that harnessing the Falls of the James had made possible.

Then came the Tara big houses that soon proliferated along the Tidewater. The same brawn and sweat were put to work creating them as well, from the stately columns and grand staircases to the great lawns, where the belles of the new royalty could be seen strolling under the frilly little parasols they used as much for flirting as for shielding them from the sun. . . .

*M*id-August, 1983. My first week in Richmond. Classes at the university aren't scheduled to begin until the second week in September, but I decided to come and settle in beforehand. In need of a few items for the apartment I've rented near campus, I find my way downtown. The shopping done, I exit the department store only to be stopped short by the startling sight of a large group of women in great hoopskirts and beribboned bonnets approaching me down the street, all of them holding up the frilly, flirtatious little antebellum parasols.

Accompanying the women are an equal number of men in dress uniform gray, swords at their sides . . .

For a hairbreadth of a second, time reverses itself: It's no longer the early 1980s, nor am I my present-day self: a writer and an itinerant teacher of writing. Instead, I'm suddenly chattel cargo, merchandise, goods, a commodity to be bought and sold in the Bottom, or on the Manchester Docks or in a Tidewater "scrambles," where I'm lassoed in the shame of my nakedness and filth.

For a hairbreadth I'm caught in a terrifying time warp until my mind somehow recovers and *registers the word "reenactment," "a Civil War reenactment," and it's 1983 again. The Scarlett O'Hara women with the parasols, the armed men in gray, are participating in what I will soon learn is perhaps the South's most enduring ritual.*

I would spend the weeks before classes began in the campus library, taking a self-administered crash course on the Old Dominion, its defining river and its people, free and otherwise. The texts I needed were all there under the call numbers 975.5 and .6, and they offered an unvarnished account of the Commonwealth's beginnings. It was obvious the books were seldom read or consulted, given the exhumed dust that flew up from their pages once they were opened. Early Southern History was clearly not a popular subject at the university. It proved otherwise for me. Long after the semester began, and with my classes underway, I continued my private crash course in southern history, finally able to redress the truncated, once-over-lightly, deliberately sanitized version of the antebellum South that had been standard in the textbooks of my day in high school and even college.

I had never, for example, come across so much as a word in any of those pages about the "scrambles" held along the tidal James.

At long last making up for having been educationally shortchanged!

One evening, digging in the stacks, I unearthed the despised Edict of 1808:

Be it enacted, by the Senate and the House of Representatives of the United States of America in Congress assembled, that from and after the 1st day of January, 1808, it shall not be lawful to import into the United States from any of the kingdoms of Africa any Negro with the intent to be sold or to be held to service or labor . . .

The furor this caused. The trade to be halted when there was still so much work to be done! Work that needed "the strength and the sinews of the African world!" as one English wag at the time put it. And with so much money still to be made buying and selling chattel labor! Where there's a will, there's, inevitably, the proverbial way, so that the 1808 Edict notwithstanding, a way was quickly found to maintain the supply and to add to it even. The Tidewater big houses: the Shirley Plantation, the Sherwood Forest Plantation, the Flowerdew Hundred Plantation, Monticello, Mount Vernon, the Swan's Point Plantation et al. began the purposeful breeding and sale of homegrown chattel. The enterprise proved so successful that, by the mid-1800s, there was a surplus of a quarter million chattel labor and more. This posed yet another problem. Again, it was easily solved. The surplus was simply, periodically, herded by cart into Richmond Towne, where it was quickly sold in the Bottom; then, as quickly, packed into the cattle cars of the CSX Railroad and into the holds of the ships at the Manchester Docks to be railroaded and shipped due south, deep south: New Orleans. The Mississippi Delta.

The river and the railroad provided the final solution.

"*Paule! Paule! The plantations! Lee's taking me to see the plantations! I can't wait!*"

A spring day in the late 1980s. It's about nine o'clock in the morning and my editor at the time, barefoot and in her nightgown, is at the top of the stairs in the house in Richmond I've just entered. There, she's performing an excited little jig while gleefully clapping her hands. She's come down from New York to visit me as well as Lee Smith, the white southern writer who's also one of her authors, and Lee, with whom she is staying, is taking her to visit the Tidewater plantations, a tourist favorite. Unaware of their plans, I had dropped by to leave off a section of the novel I'm presently working on, only to be met by my normally poised, fifty-year-old editor, a quintessential New York type, suddenly behaving like a five-year-old who's just been promised a trip to Disneyland.

For a moment I stand there nonplussed, taking in her cute little dance; then, it's all I can do not to vault up the stairs, grab her by the arm and march her, barefoot and in her nightgown, over to the campus library and there, treating her as if she's even younger than five, force-feed her the history in the dusty texts.

Shortchanged! Although my editor has been impeccably educated (the New England Sister Colleges, the Ivy League graduate schools, etc.), it appears that, like me, she was shortchanged in certain aspects of the country's history and in need of a crash course similar to mine.

Equally appalling is the fact that my editor is Jewish. How, I wonder, would she have reacted had I announced that I was on my way to visit Dachau or Buchenwald to pay my respects to the millions who had perished there while doing the boogaloo and snapping my fingers?

Our association ended shortly thereafter.

B y now the runaway part of my mind has reached the end of the James River. The sixty-mile run down from Richmond is over, and I've finally reached historic Jamestown as well as Point Comfort, the name given to the actual landing site of that first band of English settlers in 1607. A dozen years later, Point Comfort would also, ironically, be the place where the first "scrambles" of a sort took place. The captain of a Dutch three-master, a consignment of "twenty-and-odd negroes" (lowercase "n") in the hold of his ship, put them up for sale at Point Comfort. The exact provenance of the group was uncertain. It's unlikely that they were directly from "the kingdoms of Africa"—since, at the time, the trade in chattel cargo was routed mainly from West Africa to Brazil and the Caribbean archipelago. In all likelihood the "twenty-and-odd" were probably transshipments from a Caribbean island or former property of some bankrupt West Indian planter that had been peddled up the archipelago until the Dutch ship finally reached the Atlantic shoreline and Jamestown. In any event, they were immediately put up for sale at Point Comfort. No money as such changed hands. The Dutch ship being low on provisions, the chattel were exchanged for so many sacks of corn, beans and oats, so many barrels of smoked and salted meat. The exchange concluded, the "twenty-and-odd" were quickly led off to the monumental work awaiting them as well as the eight million like them who would follow over the centuries.

" Labor Day."

Startled, my friend Virginia looks over at me. I've broken our silence again. A few minutes earlier, we had been discussing where to have a leisurely holiday lunch in downtown Richmond. Once that was decided, we had fallen silent, each of us privately taking leave of the river and the last of the morning.

"Seems to me this particular holiday needs to be more inclusive in whom it acknowledges."

"Paule . . . ?"

"All those centuries of hard back, donkeywork done gratis. When I think of that . . ."

Troubled by my tone, my friend sits around to face me fully on our stone ottoman. Virginia's face. To all appearances, it is a white woman's face. In my friend's complex genealogy, white has seemingly overwhelmed all the black in her DNA. On her maternal family tree, there had been a German grandmother, a cook in a well-to-do, late-nineteenth-century New York household, who fell in love with the family's black coachman recently up from Amelia County, Virginia. Her paternal line reaches even farther back to the son of one of the antebellum's wealthiest planters. The family still ranks among today's F.F.V.s, the First Families of Virginia, that is, the true aristocracy. Their long-ago son also figured in the whiteness that dominates my friend's bloodline. But only physically. Only in appearance.

Certainly not in Virginia's mind, heart and reading of history. Indeed, occupying a place of honor in her living room is a lovingly preserved, dim little snapshot of an elderly couple seated in front of a shotgun house that is as old and weathered as they are. The man's long John Henry legs seem to extend beyond the picture's frame, while his aged wife has clearly passed down, intact, her small, sinewy body to my friend. The couple are a Southern Gothic, and they are both as black as me. They are Virginia's great-grandparents on her mother's side, once chattel labor; then sharecroppers, once they were freed.

Virginia had taken the picture with her box camera once when visiting them as a teenager.

The snapshot of the old couple always reminds me of my West Indian grandmother, whose history was not all that different. There was a small, worn, sepia-brown photograph of her that my mother—a devoted daughter—had brought with her to America. She had kept it for luck, she said, next to her passport in her pocketbook when she landed on Ellis Island over a half century ago.

"By the way," Virginia says suddenly, "I almost forgot to tell you that while you were away there was talk again, even official talk this time, about maybe putting up a historical marker at the Manchester Docks. . . ."

She waits for my reaction.

"I wouldn't hold my breath," I say.

"Me neither, I guess," Virginia adds.

With that, we gather up our empty water bottles and the cushions we had also brought along, and with my intrepid friend once again in the lead, we start the arduous climb up the north bank, leaving behind the huge willow oak of a punkah fan, our stone ottoman and the once-pristine but now shamefully polluted and ill-used river.

I'VE KNOWN SEAS:
THE CARIBBEAN SEA

Barbados, Part I

I saw New York rise shining from the sea.
—ADRIANA VIOLA CLEMENT, SEPTEMBER 9, 1923

If it so happened that "the twenty-and-odd negroes" did, in fact, arrive at Jamestown's Point Comfort by way of the West Indies instead of directly from Africa, then the island of their provenance might well have been Barbados—Barbados being, circa 1600, as important a holding pen and transshipment point as Richmond, Virginia, would become, circa 1820, owing to a surplus at the time of locally bred chattel. A green little coral gemstone of an island situated in the lower half of the Caribbean archipelago, Barbados is considered part of the conga line of islands doing their winding dance from the Florida Keys to the tip of Venezuela. Actually, Barbados has excused itself from the dance line to sit like a lonely wallflower off to itself some distance out in the Atlantic. It is the easternmost island in the chain, a tiny outpost of 166 square miles that, geographically, is the closest point in the Caribbean to the great pregnant bulge of West Africa and the former barracoon slave pens at Goree, Guinea, Elmina, Whydah, the Bight of Benin et al.

When the trade in chattel cargo began in earnest, diminutive Barbados was invariably the first bit of terra firma sighted on the long, grueling Atlantic run. The island was at once landfall and a safe haven, with a natural harbor along its Caribbean coastline. Thus, it was often the place where the chattel cargo—those that had somehow managed to survive the crossing—were prepared for market, first cleansed of the caked shit, then fed—force-fed if necessary—to put flesh on the wasted, festering limbs, and the will and spirit further broken. Once this was done—and it could take weeks—the better part of the cargo was then transshipped for sale up and down the hemisphere. Left behind was a portion needed to work the ever-expanding fields of tobacco ("the jovial weed" again) and, later on, the great sugarcane estates that would supplant tobacco to overrun Barbados. Then there were the incorrigibles, those among the consignment who somehow withstood the whipping post and the pillory, their resistance unbroken. Difficult to sell, they, too, were left behind on the little wallflower island.

Barbados, British-owned and colonized from the beginning, was a principal way station at the outset of the trade.

It was also the birthplace of my parents, descendants perhaps of the incorrigibles left behind. (I like to think as much.) My mother, Adriana Viola Clement, grew up in a hilly district called Scotland on the Atlantic or windward coast, while my father, Sam Burke, who totally disowned "the damn little two-by-four island," never mentioned either his family or the name of his birthplace, aside from referring to it, when pressed, as "some poor-behind little village buried in a sea of canes, a place forgotten behind God's back." Shortly after World War I, along with scores like them from other English-speaking islands in the Caribbean, Adriana Viola Clement and Sam Burke immigrated north to Big America. Although separately. They didn't know each other as yet.

Adriana Clement was eighteen. A photograph of her when she first arrived in New York revealed a sweet-faced girl with a childish appearance that was at odds with her tall, large-boned, fully fleshed woman's body. Physically, Adriana took after her father, Prince Albert Clement, a John Henry workhorse of a man who died when she was a child. A master cooper on one of the sugar estates, Prince Albert's sole weakness had been the rum that went into the huge casks he skillfully fashioned by hand. Adriana, as one of the youngest of his fourteen children, had been pampered growing up. Indeed, she had left Barbados not knowing how to braid her own hair. Her eldest sister, who practically raised her, had always done that for her.

The SS *Nerissa* brought her north, a leaky old tub that, according to Adriana, must have been in existence "ever since Man said, 'Come, let us make boats.'" It was a slow, turbulent journey up the Caribbean Sea that kept her, she said, "puking and praying," and clinging to the sepia-brown photograph of her mother.

"All the same, I reach safe, yes. I saw New York rise shining from the sea."

Whenever Adriana recalled the sight of the city emerging from the Atlantic, she always slowly raised her hands, palms up, like a conductor motioning a symphonic orchestra to its feet.

The soaring wonder of New York City! That first day, amid the throngs from Europe on Ellis Island ("White people like peas! And not one of them speaking the King's English": Adriana's scathing comment); that day she had presented her papers to the authorities, along with the "show money" required of those emigrating from the Caribbean. She would later explain "the show money" to her American-born children: "If you was from the West Indies you had to have fifty big

U.S. dollars to show to the authorities when you landed, to prove you wasn't a pauper or coming to the country to be a pauper. Back then, if you was black, you cun [couldn't] set foot in big America without fifty dollars cold cash in you' hand."

The "show money," as well as the much larger sum that had paid her passage north, had come from a single source: Panama Money from an older brother she had never really known. It was money so named after the canal, begun in 1905, that he had helped build. While she was still an infant, her brother, Joseph Fitzroy Clement, the eldest son, had been among the legion of young men from the islands who, hearing of the money to be made on the canal, had eagerly left for the isthmus; there to work from the time God's sun rose till it set, hacking away at the near-impenetrable jungle, draining the huge pestilential swamps, carving a waterway to link the two great oceans. A hellhole of mud, torrential rains and brutal sun, with temperatures at 120 degrees well before noon. Close to 5,000 would die over the course of the construction. Malaria. Yellow fever. Bubonic plague. The plague eventually claimed Joseph Fitzroy, but not before he dutifully sent home the better part of his pay during his years there. So, too, did most of the other islanders.

The remittances were known as Panama Money—and they were largely responsible for what might be called the West Indian wing of black America's Great Migration North, the momentous exodus that, figuratively speaking, saw "a black million-man march" from the South to the northern cities of America in the early twentieth century. During that same period, 1900 to 1925, more than 300,000 islanders, mainly from the English-speaking Caribbean, most of them Barbadians—or Bajans (pronounced Bay-gins), as they called themselves—also emigrated to the States, settling mainly in northern cities along the eastern seaboard: New York (i.e., Harlem, but even more so Brooklyn), New Haven, Hartford, Boston.

The West Indian wing of the Great Migration North could not have taken place without Panama Money.

In the Clement family, the dutiful remittances from Joseph Fitzroy were used to purchase small plots of sugarcane—or "canepieces," as they were called. These were usually rented out until one of the Clement children, or later grandchildren, was of an age to travel. A "canepiece" would then be sold to pay his or her passage to America, England or Canada.

In charge of the entire operation was Adriana's mother. She was both the "Chancellor of the Exchequer" in charge of the Panama Money as well as the architect and administrator of the "canepiece" plan. Her name: Alberta Jane Clement, née Sobers, an Alberta who had married a man named Prince Albert Clement, had borne him fourteen children, nine of whom had lived; who for years had struggled mightily with her husband over the rum drinking, and then, when he died, had gone on to outlive him by decades. Her children called her M' Da-duh, a pet name that on their lips became an honorific title. They said "M' Da-duh" the way a commoner bowing before royalty instinctively knows to say, "M' Lord," "M' Lady."

M' Da-duh inspired that kind of deference.

I met her only once. I was seven, my sister four years older, when M' Da-duh, then in her eighties, wrote to Adriana saying that her last wish before closing her eyes on the world was to see her "American-born grands." She had already sold a good-sized canepiece to pay for our passage, she wrote. The money for the tickets was on its way. Adriana was to bring us forthwith. My father had opposed the trip: "Wasting good money going back to that damn place!" For his part, he would have made some excuse to the old woman and saved the money she sent to do "something big" in America.

Adriana, the dutiful daughter, ignored him, and we set sail.

Only fragmented memories remain of the crowded disembarkation shed at Bridgetown, the capital of Barbados. However, what remains vivid in my mind is the sight of the small, resoundingly black old woman bearing down on us in a long-skirted dress that was the same blinding white as the tropical sunlight outside. Ever fresh in my memory also is the way my mother suddenly came to attention like a lowly private before a general at *the approach of her mother. The crowd in the shed even seemed to part like the Red Sea in my Sunday School book to make way for the juggernaut figure of the old woman. M' Da-duh. Decades later, still taken with her authority, I would write a story about her and her island world. Indeed, she appears, in one guise or another, in every book I've written.*

On hand to meet Adriana when she landed at age eighteen in New York was an older brother, Winston Carlyle Clement, whom M' Da-duh, using Panama Money, had sent north immediately after World War I. Practical, responsible, hardworking, a good Bajan determined to progress, Winston Carlyle had quickly established himself in Brooklyn—first, with a job in a mattress factory, where he had every intention of becoming a supervisor; he had then found himself a wife, an equally hardworking girl from home, who was also eager to progress. Moreover, Winston Carlyle was truly his mother's child in his ability to take charge and organize the lives of others. Consequently, he lost no time in finding work for Adriana. In less than a month after her arrival, the overgrown baby who didn't even know how to braid her hair found herself on Long Island cleaning the ten-room house of a white lady she was to call "Madam." She served as a nursemaid for the Madam's three small children, as well as tending to the Madam's sickly old mother. The Madam was even "learning" her how to cook like white people. The work hard, the nights though were harder still. Evenings found her relegated to a basement room without so much as a fly for company.

Many a night, head buried under the pillow to mute the sound, Adriana bawled for family and home. . . .

Until two years into the sleep-in job, when, on one of her Sundays off, she met up with one Sam Burke, a fella from home, at her brother's place in Brooklyn. Over the two years she had met a few other fellas from home, friends her brother had invited by the house. She hadn't felt anything one way or another about any of them. But this Sam Burke had a smile, a kind of playful, sure-of-himself "town" way of speaking and dressing and carrying himself. In truth, you would think he was somebody born and raised in big Bridgetown back home.

Right off Adriana took a liking to him.

Sam Burke was an illegal alien. No passport, no visa, no documents or official papers of any kind, not even a birth certificate. Moreover, he'd had no need for the fifty dollars "show money," since he'd never passed through Ellis Island. Rather, Sam Burke was a stowaway who had reached New York by way of Cuba. There had been no Panama Money to legally finance his passage north. Nor had there been any known relatives already settled in the States who might have been willing to sponsor him. He was just another bare-behind, chigger-foot country boy destined for a life cutting canes for pennies on an island that had been transformed by then into little else than a sugar bowl to sweeten England's tea.

So that desperate for a chance, any chance, Sam Burke had turned to the contract-labor scheme that occasionally sent young men like himself from the smaller islands to work for a limited time on the larger ones in the archipelago. Sam Burke signed up, was chosen, and wound up

in Cuba, in Oriente Province, where to his surprise most of the people were as black as him.
Cubans, speaking Spanish, singing Spanish, dancing Spanish, their names Spanish, but their skin
sometimes blacker than his. The work? Unhap-
pily, it was the same damn thing he had fled: cutting canes from dawn till dusk and on a plantation
twice the size of the whole of little Barbados. *The
work hard.* The machete he wielded sometimes
sending the tough slivers of cane-skin piercing his
own skin worse than the crown of thorns on Jesus'
head! The Cuban sun hotter than all the fires of
hell burning together one time! At least in little
miserable two-by-four Barbados, there were the
trade winds to once in a while cool you' skin.

Occasionally, in a reprieve from the canefields,
Sam Burke was allowed to help in transporting the
raw sugar from the plantation mill to the seaport
of Nuevitas. He loved this part of the work, loved
even more the port city of Nuevitas, the Spanish
kind of life abounding in the place. What attracted
him even more about Nuevitas was that its many
docks were always crowded with freighters, their
holds being filled with tons of raw sugar. Once

loaded, nearly all of the ships, he learned, headed due north. Their destination? The big Domino Sugar Refinery—the biggest in the world. *And sitting there in New York's harbor-self!*

Sam Burke waited good till he saw his chance.

He reached safely. And in short order found a job in a mattress factory in Brooklyn. Not long after, he met up on a Sunday with one Adriana Viola Clement, sister of a fella who was a supervisor on the job. She was a sweet-faced Bajan girl with good solid flesh on her bones and nice ways about her.

Right off he took a liking to her—and she to him, he could tell.

"But why you does call yourself Sam and not Samuel? And what's your middle name?" Adriana might have asked when she was less shy with him.

And Sam Burke might have said with a dismissive wave of his hand, "Middle name! I forget that long since! Bajans believe in having too many long, old-time English names. I decide to modernize mine. Sam Burke is all the name I need."

"Wait, you sure you ain' from Bridgetown?" Teasing him.

He laughed, pleased. "People did say that about me from when I was small, y'know. 'That boy! He gets on like somebody raise up in big Bridgetown-self.'"

Acting the part of a town blade, Sam Burke might have then abruptly changed the conversation. "But you know, you got some sweet, sweet flesh on you' bones." His mouth to her ear. His hand reaching for the sweetness.

"Wait, where you goin'? You's too forward!"

"You must tell me to stop then."

Adriana probably gave a loud suck-teeth to register her disapproval, but might not have said a word.

There remains a standard studio photograph of Adriana and Sam Burke taken shortly after the birth of their first child. Adriana, seated with the baby on her lap, is wearing a cream-colored flapper dress, a long strand of fake pearls and the de rigueur headband around her neatly combed-out hair. Dangling from her arm is an extravagantly large English garden-party hat—in all likelihood a prop supplied by the photo studio to enhance her outfit. The baby on her lap is a pretty little

girl-child (my older sister), a love child, con-
ceived some months before the marriage vows.
(A fact that would come to light only after Adriana's death.) She's holding the baby's tiny hands
in her own, and with quiet pride offers the camera not only the sight of her perfect child but herself as well, someone who has been rescued from
cleaning a ten-room house on Long Island and is
now a wife, a mother and a Madam in her own
right. And with her own home, if you please!
True, it's only a cold-water flat in Red Hook,
Brooklyn, up with the Eye-talians who can scarce
speak a word of English. True, the bathtub is
right in the middle of the kitchen. But never
mind. Like all Bajans she and her new husband
are looking to do better, determined to progress.

Beside her in the photograph stands Sam
Burke, his thick bush of hair parted boldly down
the middle above his sharply planed, long-jawed,
handsome face. He, too, is dressed for the occasion, in a three-piece suit that, although cheap,
looks expensive on him, even custom made. A
boulevardier's bow tie complements the bespoke-
looking suit, as does the handkerchief and fountain

Adriana and Sam Burke (and their firstborn),
Brooklyn, 1925

pen in his breast pocket. One hand is thrust into his trouser pocket. His other hand holds a cane (probably also a studio prop) angled just so at his side.

Sam Burke presents himself as someone who has never been near a canefield, or, for that matter, inside a damn mattress factory where he has to wear a snood like a woman to protect his hair from the lint flying about the place. The ignominy of that snood! No, Sam Burke has never been near a field or a factory in his life! The haughty gaze he directs at the camera dares it to reveal otherwise.

That was his way. My father went about life insisting, by his manner, that his was a higher calling than the series of factory jobs he held over the years. In his eyes he possessed the ability and talent to be so much more. . . .

The course he took in radio repair—which he never finished—almost ruined our priceless secondhand console radio in the living room. Once he abruptly discontinued a home-study course he was taking in accounting. Too damn long, too many figures, too expensive. The trumpet lessons that went on every Saturday and Sunday morning for months kept us with our hands clapped over our ears until the trumpet, too, was abandoned.

Also, on and off for years, he was a salesman after work and on weekends. Sample case in hand, cheap suit fitting him just so, he made the rounds of black Brooklyn selling a variety of products not to be found in the white department stores downtown. One time it was hair grease and hot combs; then a line of cosmetics compatible with the dark skin of his customers; later on, ladies' hose in a monochrome of brown. These and other selling ventures Sam Burke pursued until they either failed to turn a profit or he simply grew tired of repeating the sales pitch: "Each time you singing the same damn tune just to sell a pair of stockings. Finish with that!" Or—and this was more often the case—he had again decided that selling door-to-door was beneath his talents.

Although the holy grail of his true calling continued to elude him, Sam Burke remained surprisingly optimistic. A vocation that truly suited him? A job that didn't call for the overalls and work clothes of a common laborer? It was only a matter of time. So that, especially with me and my sister, he remained his playful, irresistible "Bridgetown" self.

"Ladyfolks, ladyfolks, rise and shine and give God the glory!" was the way he roused us each morning. While in Cuba he had fallen in love with all things Spanish and had named us accordingly: Anita for my sister; Valenza, after Valencia, for me—although I was called by my middle name, Pauline. (A name I promptly changed to Paule with a silent "e" the moment I reached my majority at age thirteen.) Among the few Spanish words and phrases our father had retained was *"Quieta la boca"*—so that he loved it when our noisy sibling rivalry gave him an excuse to cry out, *"Señoritas, señoritas, quieta la boca, por favor!"*

He sang. Whenever Adriana complained about his frequent job changes and the abandoned mail-order courses and selling ventures, Sam Burke would drown her out with song. It was always the same song, a hymn he might have learned as a boy in the little poor-behind village forgotten behind God's back that he refused to name, a hymn like a Gregorian chant being sung in the high stone nave of a cathedral. *"Satan go 'way / Satan go 'way / Satan go 'way / And let Jesus come in,"* he would intone repeatedly to silence the Beelzebub of her voice.

It usually worked. Adriana would eventually throw up her arms in loving despair and cease complaining.

My own personal and fondest memory of Sam Burke and his antic ways has to do with a soft-boiled egg. A child who was slow to talk, I had been left in his care one morning, with instructions that I was to be fed my usual soft-boiled egg for breakfast. Initially, he went about preparing the egg the proper way: briefly boiling it, then emptying the white and yolk into the eggcup; next, a pinch of salt, a smidgen of butter. But then, instead of using a spoon to stir the mixture, Sam Burke reached for one of the extra long wooden matches used to light the coal stove that was our source for both cooking and heat. Smiling, holding the match by its flammable head, he waved the long stick like a magician's wand before abruptly using it to stir my egg. I shook my head no and kept on shaking it even as he continued stirring with the matchstick, until magically, the egg became a frothy albuminous yellow. Which was exactly the way I liked it. Only then did he pick up the spoon to feed me.

To this day it remains the best soft-boiled egg I've ever eaten.

As an illegal, Sam Burke lived in constant fear of the INS: Any day, undocumented alien that he was, he could be found out, arrested, jailed and deported. He was nonetheless fiercely patriotic and, during the war—World War II—he must have wanted to express his loyalty in some public, tangible way. Because one Saturday morning, Sam Burke marched his two girl-children, his ladyfolks, his señoritas, to downtown Brooklyn, and blowing his entire week's pay, bought us both U.S. Air Force bomber jackets.

How he must have wanted a boy-child! True, Sam Burke loved me no less for being a girl. Yet my birth, coming four long years after my sister's, must have been something of a disappointment for him, if only briefly.

It was a grievous and permanent disappointment for Adriana. This I knew before I even fought my way out of her womb. Because hadn't I, during my nine months there, heard her praying nonstop for a boy-child, Adriana believing that a little Sam Burke, Jr., would miraculously transform his father into a provider on the order of her brother, Winston Carlyle, and the other Bajan men who were all steadily progressing in spite of "the discrimination n' thing in this man country." Adriana had pinned her hopes on a birth she was certain would produce the needed sea change in her husband.

Imagine then her disappointment at yet another girl-child; and one, at that, who was nothing as pretty as her first. From early on, Adriana would recite almost daily the list of my physical flaws: my large, bright-pink lower lip ("like a piece o' raw meat"); my two ugly, oversized big toes; "the two horse teeth" that replaced my milk teeth up front. As for my gloomy, long-jawed face? It was the face, according to Adriana, "of a child that's living its old days first!"

There were my personality flaws as well:

"Hard-ears!"

"Willful!"

"Own-ways!"

And I did, indeed, pretty much go my own way almost from the beginning. So that in the formal studio photograph that is taken of every Bajan child by age five—even of those children like myself who are disappointments—my picture revealed an unsmiling, rather severe-looking four-year-old whose hands were firmly clasped on top of the children's picture book she'd been given as a prop.

Willful, own-ways, I had also already chosen my life's work.

Although I wasn't the hoped-for miracle worker, we did manage to graduate from the cold-water flats in Red Hook and on Fulton Street where I was actually born. We then lived in a series of walkups that at least had steam heat, hot water, a gas stove, and the bathtub where it naturally belonged. Later, when the white flight began in force from the uptown, upscale, tree-lined neighborhoods of Bedford and Stuyvesant Heights in central Brooklyn, where a few Bajans, including Adriana's always-progressing brother, had already succeeded in purchasing a number of the prized brownstone houses, we, too, the Burke family, also managed to make the move to "the heights." Our circumstances hadn't really improved, yet with Adriana supplementing Sam Burke's weekly salary by doing day's work—the Madams again—we were able to lease an old Victorian brownstone on Hancock Street uptown.

No. 501 Hancock was a plain Jane of a brownstone with almost no decorative stonework on its somber reddish-brown four-story façade. It was graced, however, by a handsome chestnut tree out front, a pear tree in the backyard, a sun parlor on the second floor that overlooked the pear tree, and two upper-floor apartments that could be rented out to pay the greater part of the lease.

Best of all for me, 501 Hancock was only a short distance from a local branch of the Brooklyn Public Library. A necessary home away from home. It was there, come age twelve, that I summoned up the courage one day to ask the white librarian for a list of books by colored writers.

"Books! Books! Her middle name is books!" is the way Adriana greeted me each time I returned

from the library with an armload. "Her head always buried in a book!"

For his part, Sam Burke claimed as his domain at 501 the sun parlor with its sheer wall of windows flooded with light. He spent his weekends there, recovering from the factory job of the moment, while dreaming up other pursuits that might free him from such jobs.

As for Adriana, her realm was the large kitchen on the ground floor where she entertained her friends, part-time day-workers like herself and all of them women from home. Bajans seldom socialized with the other islanders who had also immigrated to Brooklyn. Trinidadians were considered too frivolous, a people who lived only for their yearly carnival. Jamaicans in their view were a rough lot who disgraced the King's English by dropping their "h's" ('im dis and 'im dat). Those from the lesser-known islands such as St. Vincent, Grenada, St. Lucia and the like were dismissed as "low-islanders," meaning small, insignificant. As for American black people, they needed to stand up more to the white man. Bajans, meanwhile, had no objection to being called "the Jews of the

West Indies" by the other islanders—the term based on their perceived ability "to squeeze a penny till it cried 'Murder! Murder!'" and "to turn a dime into a dollar overnight." There was their known entrepreneurial chutzpah in general: "As soon as a Bajan gets ten cents above a beggar he opens a business."

The tight, insular little world of Bajan Brooklyn took pride in the stereotypes attributed to it.

Whenever Adriana and her friends gathered in the kitchen to "ol' talk," as they put it, my sister and I, as girl-children, were required to be on hand, seen but not heard. Those times were the happiest I ever saw Adriana. In their highly inventive Bajan English, she and her "soully-gal" friends from home talked about everything under the sun and had an opinion about everything. What I loved most were the sayings and Bajan proverbs that embellished their endless talk. Most I didn't understand fully, but loved anyway.

"I tell yuh, I has read hell by heart and called every generation blessed!" This when overwhelmed by trouble of one kind or another.

"The sea ain' got no back door!" Caution. The importance of exercising caution in this life. "If you's caught in a house that's on fire there's a chance maybe to escape through the back door. Not so the sea. No back doors."

"Beautiful-ugly." Their favorite adjective for nearly everything, including even the brownstones they were desperately struggling to buy or simply to lease. "The beautiful-ugly old house. Is nothing but trouble." Everything for them contained its opposite.

"Cut-and-contrive." "I tell yuh, in this life you got to know how to cut-and-contrive." Improvisation. One had to know how to improvise to survive.

The mothers were skillful raconteurs as well. A few among them, including Adriana, were acknowledged to be superlative talkers and master storytellers. Those few were crowned "mout'-kings," kings of "talking the talk," as it were.

"Soully-gal, you's a real-real mout'-king!" was said of them.

There was no greater compliment.

I couldn't have known it at the time, but I had my first lessons in the art and craft of writing while being forced to listen to Adriana and her friends in the kitchen at 501 Hancock. Decades later, I would christen them the "Mother Poets" and pay grateful homage to them in an article called "The Poets in the Kitchen," which was published as part of a series on the "Making of a Writer" in the *New York Times Sunday Book Review*.

"Every Bajan buying and we still leasing! Shame! I feel so shame I don' even like going 'round my friends or family anymore, especially that brother of mine, what with that wife of his always showing off all the nice-nice things they have just so's to make me feel bad. I can't stand the sight of that woman!

"Shame! That I went and put myself with somebody you'd never think was a Bajan. No real get-up-and-go to him a-tall. Always trying out one foolish scheme after another that don' turn so much as a penny! Shame!"

Adriana's Xanthippe voice in 501's austere, high-ceilinged rooms. Over the years the sweet-faced young mother in the family photograph had become a West Indian version of Socrates' shrewish wife.

Also, by then, Sam Burke had long abandoned trying to silence her with his playful "Satan go 'way" hymn. Now, pitting his voice against hers, he equally assailed her for having squandered the Panama Money years ago on the visit home. Money that could have been a down payment on the "beautiful-ugly" house—said with the utmost sarcasm—that she so craved. Finally, he ceased responding in kind. Rather, when the Xanthippe voice became unbearable, Sam Burke simply put on one of his cheap, bespoke-looking suits and took to the streets. Or, according to Adriana, "took to his latest 'keep-miss,'" some woman who, like herself long ago, could not resist the bold part down the middle of his hair, his "Bridgetown ways," his abbreviated, modernized name, and his charm.

At last, a boy-child. Nine years after my disappointing birth, the long-hoped-for son finally, his name Franklin Edsel, after FDR and the car maker Henry Ford's only child. Fate being what it is, however, the boy-child arrived too late to bring about any miracles, because by then Sam Burke, in his endless seeking, had found god. God in the person of a short, brown, bald and rotund fellow named George Baker from Georgia, who, having migrated north, had somehow metamorphosed into a god called Father Divine, with his heavenly kingdom an old, outsized brownstone mansion in Harlem. Moreover, this *Father* Divine declared himself to be the one and only father to his followers, the Sole Progenitor, the Divine Paterfamilias. Consequently, all his followers were his children. So that no matter what had once been their familial roles, they were now, in effect, brothers or sisters to their so-called spouses, and to their so-called children as well.

Thus Sam Burke, our father, became Brother Burke. His worshipful daughters, his long-awaited son, his wife, all were to think of him as their brother and to address him as such: Brother Burke. The short little self-proclaimed god from Georgia had relieved him of the onus of being both husband and father.

"Thank you, Father Divine. Peace, it's truly wonderful. Father will provide."

This became Sam Burke's principal mantra, intoned almost nonstop. His gaze also assumed the otherworldly cast of an adept, while an almost visible aura seemed to have formed around him, rendering him immune to the abuse Adriana heaped equally on him and on his "little dough-off [meaning 'short'], bald-head, so-called god."

Adriana verbally assaulted them both without letup to the day that her husband (now "brother") quit his latest factory job and proudly announced that Father Divine had chosen him to help administer a branch of the kingdom being established in Philadelphia.

His so-called god had delivered him at last from the long futile search for a vocation worthy of his still undefined talents.

"Thank you, Father. Peace, it's truly wonderful. Father will provide."

With that, Brother Burke, a.k.a. Sam Burke, vanished from our lives, leaving behind among his discarded family a devastated eleven-year-old.

With him gone, whatever small gains we had made were quickly lost, beginning with 501 Hancock. Even with the rent from the two upper floors, Adriana simply could not manage the lease. Nor would she ask her brother for help, having broken off all contact with him due to his wife, whom she despised, the woman forever boasting of her nice-nice things. There were other family members in England and Canada, but they were of no help. So that in short order we returned to the series of walkups, even cheaper ones this time. Even so, we often found ourselves about to be evicted for back rent, our belongings piled on the sidewalk. We became nomads wandering from one brief resting place to another in central Brooklyn until we finally ended up in the cramped third-floor apartment of a brownstone owned by a fellow Bajan.

The ultimate humiliation for Adriana.

With Sam Burke gone, she also spent hours, sometimes an entire day, putting us, her adolescent daughters, on guard against his kind. In warnings that were also threats, Adriana spelled out, in Bajan English that sounded almost Elizabethan (straight from the pit of the Globe Theatre), the dire consequences that awaited us should we become "little wring-tail concubines caterwauling about the streets looking for men." Or worse, should we ever come before her with our stomachs "tumbling big with some wild-dog puppy." Again shaming her before every Bajan in Brooklyn. Oh, no, we would have to pack our little "georgie-bundles" (Elizabethan for suitcases), take our little wild-dog puppy and *"Get from out my eyesight!"*

Adriana threatening banishment in an effort to save us from a fate similar to her own. And she went about it the only way she knew how, using the Xanthippe voice that by now had become a force greater than herself.

Barbados, Part II

"College?! Book writing?! Look, get from out my eyesight! You ain' hear that the telephone company is starting to hire colored? You best march yourself down there and beg for a job!"

Adriana promoted the telephone company nonstop. But to no avail. Because by then, at age seventeen, I had quietly enrolled in Hunter College, which was free at the time to all New York City residents, once your grades qualified. By then I had also found two part-time jobs at branches of the New York Public Library, in order to contribute my share at home. Above all, and again secretly, I was writing a novel on the sly, my first, and soon even progressed with it to the point of considering possible publishing houses, starting with the best known among them.

My editor at Random House, a tall, imposing New England Brahmin of a man named Hiram Haydn, slowly slid his copy of my six-hundred-page manuscript back to me across his desk.

"Okay," he said. "The contract's signed, so that's done. You've also got some 'money in your purse'—and I wish we could have given you a larger advance, but then it's a first book. And we have a title. *Brown Girl, Brownstones.* I like it. I think it'll sell. At any rate the business end of things is out of the way, and it's time now for you to get back down to work.

"And the work, dear author," he placed a large hand on top of my manuscript, "is for you to take this swollen, overwritten baby tome of yours and to extricate from it the slender, impressive first novel that's buried there. Along with the changes we've already discussed, I've attached a list of other suggestions that might help. The next phase of the work, the real work in some ways, is about to begin."

Hiram Haydn dismissed what must have been the crestfallen look on my face with a laugh that reached the ceiling in the palatial room that was his office as editor-in-chief. (Random House at the time, the mid-fifties, was headquartered in a pair of regal, neo-Renaissance buildings on Madison Avenue.)

"Don't look so worried," he said. "*You* can do it!"

Spoken with absolute confidence across the desk.

"It'll take time, of course," he added, and then went on to suggest that instead of remaining in expensive New York I should go someplace where the modest advance would better buy the time I needed to get the revisions done.

"Barbados."

I didn't even have to think.

Hiram Haydn solemnly nodded. "Yes," he said, "from this book of yours I think it's important that you go there."

With that decided, the moment I left his office I took the subway downtown to Delancey Street on the Lower East Side and the sprawling indoor/outdoor Jewish market there that was known as the poor man's Macy's in New York. After the ritual haggling over the price with the Orthodox shopkeepers in their yarmulkes and oversized black fedoras, I bought—cheap—two extra-large suitcases that might actually have been genuine leather as the salesman claimed.

I was living in Manhattan by then, and the moment I reached my apartment uptown I started packing for the trip.

I was also married by then—both my sister and I driven into early marriages by the daily harangues about "caterwauling," "wild-dog puppies" and the like. Marriage would pose no problem, though, to my taking off to the Caribbean to write. My husband was also someone in flight from the insular world of Bajan Brooklyn, where his family owned several brownstones. Ours was a mutual apostasy that also rejected traditional marriage, so that while we lived together, slept together, we essentially led fairly independent, unfettered lives. An open marriage, as it were. We were only in our early twenties, after all. Truthfully, even when we finally had a child some nine years later (the book-party baby that arrived with the publication of that first novel), I still wasn't suited for the settled, stay-at-home married life. And this eventually, inevitably, led to a divorce.

Portable typewriter in one hand, overweight manuscript in the other and the two Delancey Street suitcases in tow, I left for Barbados in a matter of days, there to remain for almost a year. On a practical level it was the right choice. Tourism had not as yet descended on the little wallflower island off by itself in the Atlantic, so that my modest advance had almost the exchange rate of gold when compared to the local dollar. The other and more important reason for choosing Barbados was, of course, Adriana and Sam Burke. Perhaps living in their birthplace might help me to better understand them—and understanding might, in turn, bring about the forgiveness I as yet could not fully give.

With my American dollars, I quickly found room and board in a large, newly built manor-style house near the capital, Bridgetown, on the Caribbean, or leeward, side of the island. The owner of the house was a somewhat dour, taciturn old Bajan, a bachelor who had retired back home after fifty years spent working two jobs in Hartford, Connecticut, where he had also acquired considerable rental property. Once back in Barbados he had used his life's savings to build this replica of a white planter's great house, exhausting, it's said, all his savings in the process. In fact, his grudging willingness to have me as a boarder was to help with the upkeep the place required. Mr. Watson was his name. In his youth he would not have dared to set foot near a house such as the one he now possessed—except, perhaps, to beg for a job as a yard boy.

I would later write a story about old Mr. Watson and his colonial showpiece. It would be part of a collection of stories about old men called *Soul Clap Hands and Sing,* the title taken from a poem by W. B. Yeats on the subject of aging.

Once settled, I got down to work overhauling the bloated baby tome of a novel. Using Hiram Haydn's notes and suggestions, as well as my own instincts, I began eliminating what I soon came to see were the excesses burdening the narrative, impeding its pace. All that highly decorative prose that called attention to itself! Style overwhelming rather than serving the story! Worst was the surfeit of details! Three or more qualifiers to describe an object when one alone would do! Long hours were spent painstakingly cutting away the fat. Some days the revising felt like a wrestling match that had unfairly pitted me, a rank amateur, against an opponent, my sumo-sized manuscript, that was far superior in weight, strength and skill. It was somehow up to me, the underdog, the weakling, to pin the behemoth to the mat and strip it of every superfluous word.

Days—long, solitary days, weeks and then months spent learning the painful but necessary lesson of every novice: that writing is rewriting, is honing, pruning, refining, is becoming, essentially, one's own unsparing editor.

At times when the work became too punishing or I simply needed a break from the loneliness and the routine, I would flee Mr. Watson's plantation house and treat myself to a swim—or what the local folk called "a sea-bath." Bajans never used the word "swim." Rather, on Sunday mornings usually, an entire family might go for a sea-bath, with everyone swimming but also standing and washing themselves down in the surf, especially the older folk. According to them, "a sea-bath" in the waters surrounding their little coral gemstone of an island had the power to heal whatever ailed you. I could have used those healing powers years earlier when I came down briefly with tuberculosis while at Hunter College, the disease brought on in part by my taking a full academic program while working two part-time jobs. All this on a diet that consisted of little else than sandwiches eaten on the run.

It was still better than the telephone company.

In Barbados, as relief from the writing, I also spent time at the Museum and Historical Society, reading up on the early history of the island. Other times, needing company, I sought out the small group of friends I had made once I settled in. They were all part of the pro-independence movement slowly getting underway on the island, young barristers, doctors, economists and other professionals, the lucky few who had won island scholarships to study in England: the Inns of Court, King's College, Cambridge, the London

School of Economics. To a man, they had re-turned home radicalized and eager for change.

"Look at Ghana, man! I hear it gon soon be in-dependent! So why not us? What the bloody hell wrong with us, nuh? We Bajans need to tear down all the blasted pictures of the queen, then chase her kiss-me-ass governor-general out of Govern-ment House and run Barbados on we own! It's we country, nuh! Is we sweat and blood build the place!"

Long, heated discussions during which they reverted to pure Bajanese. How I envied them! Black people who could actually anticipate taking charge politically! Who could seriously contem-plate running their own government! What black American could ever dream of exercising that kind of power?

As for Barbados, it would be another nine years later, in 1966, before it finally achieved in-dependence. And even then the old colonial imprimatur—economically, culturally, socially—would remain intact for some time.

At least twice a month, I dutifully traveled up to the remote hilly district called Scotland on the

Atlantic side of the island where Adriana had been born, there to visit her eldest sister and the only one of the Clement children who still remained on the island. Her name: Branford Catherine. Adriana always wrote to her and, whenever she could afford it, would slip a five- or ten-dollar remittance in the letter. After all, Branford Catherine had been her surrogate mother, the one who had braided her hair up to the day she set sail for America.

The trip up to the Scotland District began in Bridgetown, which at the time was your typical small island colonial capital, with the long-established white planter and merchant class, their heirs and descendants, still controlling every aspect of the commercial life in the place. Adjoining a large open-air market near the edge of town was the equally large outdoor bus stand where the country buses assembled for their scheduled runs to the various districts or parishes on the island.

"Mints. Toffees. Nuts. Who call?"

"Julie mangoes. Sweet-to-you'-mout' Julie mangoes. Who call?"

"Sweet drinks: Fanta. Juice-C. Cola. Ice-cold! Who call?"

The cries of the women hawkers plying their snacks among the buses waiting to depart called to mind Adriana and her "mout'-king" friends at 501 Hancock Street. So, too, did the hawkers' faces under the heavy trays of candies and fruit and the heavier basins of sodas and ice they carried seemingly effortlessly on their heads.

"Mints. Toffees. Nuts. Who call?"

I usually bought a piece of fruit and a cold soda.

The country buses were makeshift affairs completely open on the sides, the only protection when it rained being a length of tarpaulin that could be lowered from the roof. Rows of benches nailed to the floor provided the seating. Then there were the drivers, the younger ones especially, who behaved as if the jury-rigged vehicles were prime entries in the Indianapolis 500. Keeping the accelerator to the floor, they sent the buses barreling headlong in what seemed a deliberate game of chicken with every oncoming bus, car, lorry (truck), bicycle and donkey cart. Complaints from the passengers (and they complained often and loud) were treated as compliments by the madcap at the wheel.

For an hour or more we traversed a Barbados that felt larger than its minuscule 160-odd square miles. Creating the illusion of greater size were the narrow, winding country roads, the villages of little tin-roofed chattel houses endlessly repeated along the roads and sugarcane fields as far and wide as the eye could see. Above all, there was the seeming overflow of humanity everywhere. "Bajans like peas," Adriana would have said. Indeed, Barbados remains the eighth most densely populated piece of real estate on earth.

The Scotland District finally, so named probably by some "poor johnny" Scotsman long ago nostalgic for his native Highlands. But "Scotland" was a misnomer when applied to the few low, nondescript limestone hills crowded into the northeast corner of the otherwise flat island. Chalk-white some of them, the hills surrounded the valley floor where my eighty-five-year-old aunt, Branford Catherine, lived in a two-room board-and-shingle house, weathered dun-gray by the sun. The house stood on the Clement family's last remaining "canepiece," the one that would have been sold to finance Branford Catherine's passage north had she not defied her mother, the imperious M' Da-duh, and refused to emigrate.

I had no recollection of my aunt from the childhood visit years before. Nor did the old woman remember me, given that she was almost completely senile. Long-legged, large-boned, her body apparently still fit, her black face still miraculously unlined, but her mind eclipsed. Branford Catherine spent her days on an old-fashioned wooden recliner called a planter's chair in the tiny sitting room of her house. There she was devotedly cared for by a niece of her late husband.

The niece, called simply Mis' Edith, was a sprightly middle-aged spinster who delighted in repeating the saga of my aunt's life whenever I came to visit. Not only had the young Branford Catherine refused to be sent north, she had also chosen to become a common hawker, to M' Da-duh's shame and disgust. According to Mis' Edith, dawn would find Branford Catherine, a full basket of mangoes, yams, cassava and the like on her head, briskly setting out on the fourteen-mile walk to the main market in Bridgetown. Hawking—buying and selling, commerce—had been her life and her love. Even now, on those rare occasions when, as Mis' Edith put it, "she comes back to she-self for a minute, her mind clear-clear as a bell"—when that happened Branford Catherine was known to slip out of the house and set off down the road to the main market in Bridgetown.

"I has to watch she like a hawk."

I once witnessed one of those fleeting resurrections. My aunt, moribund on her planter's chair, suddenly turned one day to where I was sitting nearby and, peering at me, said "Adrie?" (Adrie had been Adriana's pet name as a child.) "Is you, Adrie . . . ?" The old woman's eyes, the whites stained tobacco-brown with age, carefully parsed my face. Again: "Adrie . . . ?" Then, before I could react, her mind abruptly shut down again.

Adriana, who had recently died, would not have been pleased to learn that she and I looked so much alike.

The ironies and absurdities of my family history! A rumhead of a grandfather—a brilliant craftsman, yes, but a rumhead nonetheless—who had been named after Queen Victoria's consort. Then, a little dictator of a grandmother who had so impressed me at age seven that I would forever memorialize her in my work. An aunt who had rejected Big America to remain on the little two-by-four island as a common hawker. An uncle in Brooklyn who, having converted the several brownstones he had accumulated into rooming houses, now lived rich as Croesus on Long Island—he and the other West Indians like himself responsible, in part, for creating the near-ruin of an inner city now called "Bed-Stuy." Then there were all the other Clement family members, known and unknown, dispersed widely across England, Canada and elsewhere.

At the same time, there was the lacuna, the missing chapter in the manuscript of my life, as it were, created by Sam Burke, a man who, for whatever reasons, refused to ever speak of father, mother, sister or brother; who wouldn't even name his birthplace on the island, aside from dismissing it as "some poor-behind little village buried in a sea of canes, a place hidden, forgotten behind God's back."

The same was true of him. Everything about Sam Burke was also "hidden behind God's back," and remained so, I discovered, when I tried tracking down his family and birthplace while in Barbados. Each attempt on my part proved futile. Until, the old unforgiving anger with him flaring up again, I abandoned the search, telling myself in my bitterness that Sam Burke might not even have been his name, but an alias he had concocted out of the raw sugar in the hold of the freighter that had brought him, a stowaway, to New York.

Again furious with the father I continued helplessly to love.

Abandoning the search, I began filling in the lacuna Sam Burke represented with other, adopted "kinfolk": with, for example, "the incorrigibles" in Barbados long ago who had somehow withstood the whipping post and the pillory. I claimed them among my progenitors. Also, "the twenty-and-odd negroes" at Point Comfort, Jamestown, Virginia, who had been exchanged for so many sacks of meal and salted meat before being led off to centuries of John Henry work. Next: little Olaudah Equiano, the captured eleven-year-old boy-child from Yoruba Land who had arrived traumatized in Barbados in 1756, only to be transshipped to Point Comfort also. Years later, Equiano, the man, would write a best-selling narrative of his travails once he managed to purchase his freedom.

Then there were the 132 sick and ailing chattel cargo in the hold of the *Zong,* a British three-master bound for the Caribbean in 1781. The entire lot had been disposed of at sea, the ship owners calculating that the insurance money from the loss would be far greater than the sale of the chattel in their condition.

On reading of the Zong Massacre, as it was called, I promptly added all 132 of the drowned to my gene pool.

The bimonthly trip upcountry to Scotland always ended at a place called Bathsheba, where I caught the bus back to town. From my aunt's village, a delightfully solitary walk alongside the Atlantic led the way to Bathsheba. To my right rose the "Scottish Highlands," where the old planter and merchant class, as well as their heirs and descendants, had built large, airy summer homes whose wraparound verandas stood open to the trade winds. To my left, the Atlantic repeatedly flung its high, swollen grayish-green waves onto the shingle beach with a cry each time that might have been taken from the Book of Lamentations.

The Atlantic: an entire ocean permanently sitting shivah.

Usually accompanying me on the walk was a flock of plovers come to play a game of tag. Alighting well ahead of me up the beach, they would remain put, supposedly oblivious to my approach, until of course I drew too close for comfort. They would then dramatically take to the air, cawing, laughing, only to alight further on to await me again.

The teasing birds, the inconsolable ocean, the misnamed hills, the burning-hot Cyclops eye of the midday sun all led finally to a high rocky outcropping—a cliff really—that brought the beach and the entire shoreline to an end and deposited me at Bathsheba.

Bathsheba was the name of practically every feature of the landscape here, including the high cliff, the village adjoining the cliff where the bus stop was located, and even the modest hotel on top of the cliff, although the hotel's name was actually the "Atlantis." Its airy veranda was my watering hole after the long walk in the hot sun. I always began with a tall glass of ice water. A leisurely gin-and-tonic then followed, or, sometimes, a rum-and-ginger, "demon rum," in memoriam to Prince Albert Clement, master cooper.

Bathsheba was also the name assigned to the final stretch of beach below the hotel where several massive limestone boulders, long blackened by time, stood tall in the roiling surf. Stonehenge. The assemblage of huge rocks was a West Indian Stonehenge, I decided, whose provenance and purpose lay open to the imagination. An earthquake or a hurricane millennia ago might have dislodged them from the "Scottish" hills and sent them hurtling down to the shoreline. Or, in a superhuman show of strength, the original Amerindian or Carib dwellers of Barbados might have placed them there to ward off all invaders from the sea. And it had worked, at least here at Bathsheba, given that centuries ago, when the first merchant ship arrived from Goree or Guinea, Elmina or Whydah or the Bight of Benin, the Stonehenge barrier at Bathsheba had forced it to hightail around to leeward and the mild-mannered Caribbean to find a landing site.

Although the Scotland visits were a much-needed break from the writing, I invariably brought the work along in my head. There was much cutting, revising and fine-tuning still to be done. Moreover, part of my mind was also taken up with the next book I intended to write. This new book, another novel, was increasingly taking over my thoughts. The idea for it, the seed, had come to me literally by accident. On one of my first trips upcountry the bus I was on had been held up by an accident on the narrow country road. One of the huge lorries used to transport the harvested sugarcane to the mills had side-swiped a parked lorry being loaded at the roadside. No damage had been done; yet a full-scale shouting match was underway between the work crews on the two lorries. There was more "Gor blimmuh this, Gor blimmuh that!" (untranslatable) to be heard. More "Wha' de shite this, Wha' de rass-hole that!" Along with much posturing and displays of menacing gestures. All of it pure theater.

What interested me more than the men and their histrionics were the women "headers" at the scene. These were the women who worked in the fields during "crop-time," their job to tie the freshly cut canes into great bundles weighing hundreds of pounds, which they then carried on their heads across the fields to the lorries waiting at the roadside. This usually called for a long walk in the hot sun. A group of these women, the hundreds-weight load of canes on their heads, stood nearby angrily demanding that the crew on their lorry stop their quarreling and come help them unload. (They could neither hoist nor lower the bundled canes on their own without seriously injuring themselves.) Left ignored on the sidelines, the women, exasperated, soon also started cursing, adding their own "gor blimmuhs" to the verbal free-for-all.

One of the headers, though, remained silent. A stringy, raw-boned woman with large, badly splayed feet, she appeared to be oblivious to the shouting match around her and, strangely, even oblivious to the overload of canes on her head and the searing midday sun. Indeed, the woman seemed entirely removed from everything and everyone around her—her gaze was that distant, that detached. It was almost as if she had *physically* turned away from the present scene, the present moment, and, the huge sheaf of canes on her head, was walking back toward another place and another time altogether. Or so it seemed to me. Her unsightly feet taking her back to some past event that I imagined was of far more importance than the squabble at the roadside.

From her eager stride, it had to be a momentous event, one that had perhaps promised her and those like her something better than canefields, hot sun and work as headers during the crop season. And she, for one, would steadfastly refuse to engage the present, the here-and-now, until that long-ago promise was fulfilled. The set expression on her face declared as much.

And what might have been the momentous event to which she remained so faithful? Might it have been the Easter Sunday morning uprising of 1816 that I had read about at the Barbados Museum and Historical Society? The rebellion had been led by the legendary, the "incorrigible" Bussa (his chattel name was simply "Bussa") and his equally "incorrigible" coconspirator, the house servant Nanny Griggs. Plotting together, the two had managed to assemble a force of some four hundred and more from the surrounding plantations. Then, come Easter dawn, with the planters attending the sunrise service, the chattel forces had struck. The rebellion failed, as did many others on the island from the beginning. Nevertheless, Bussa and Nanny Griggs are considered the Nat Turner and Toussaint L'Ouverture of Barbados. They also occupy a prominent place in my improvised ancestral tree.

Years later they would also serve as inspiration for my second novel, *The Chosen Place, the Timeless People.*

Finally, after almost ten months, the revisions were done. I had achieved, I felt, a tighter, more focused, less self-indulgent manuscript. Eager to show Hiram Haydn what I had accomplished, eager also to begin the new novel I had in mind, I prepared to leave for home. The day before my flight, I went up to Scotland to say goodbye to Aunt Branford Catherine. She would have died by the time I returned to Barbados. But no matter: I would encounter her alive and well, her buying-and-selling hawker's mind completely restored, in every West Indian and African marketplace I was to visit over the coming years.

Back in town that last day, I went for a long sea-bath in the afternoon. (A farewell dinner with my pro-independence friends would follow in the evening.) This time I chose the most glorious of the beaches along the leeward coast, a seemingly endless littoral with sand a pale beige verging on white and water so pure it truly looked as if it could cure whatever ailed you.

Tragically, by my next visit, this entire coastline would have metamorphosed into an upscale version of a Miami-style beachfront, with one luxury hotel after another arrayed up its length, along with mansion-style retirement homes for the expatriate rich and famous: aging movie stars (Claudette Colbert), retired British royalty (Sir Ronald Tree). Moreover, the mansions and five-star hotels had been constructed in such a way along the coastal road that it would be virtually impossible for ordinary Bajans to gain access to the beach for a sea-bath on a Sunday morning. An entire section of the island's coastline would become off-limits to its citizens.

Thankfully, the day before my departure, the beach was still its unspoiled self and accessible to all. For a time, I did a lazy crawl close to shore, feeling unburdened for the first time in months. Then, turning over, I floated for awhile—arms outstretched, eyes closed, face raised to the sky and its huge day star—floating as if simply allowing the warm, amniotic waters of the Caribbean archipelago to take me where they willed.

The islands were to become something of a home away from home for years to come.

Grenada, 1962

When news arrived that *Brown Girl, Brownstones*, that first novel of mine, had won a Guggenheim Award, the most generous and prestigious literary prize after the famous Pulitzer, the first thing I did was to phone Mr. Hughes and again thank him for having written one of the letters of recommendation that, I'm sure, helped me to secure such a bonanza of a grant.

Next, I immediately made preparations to head back down to the West Indies. Money on the order of a Guggenheim would buy me far more time there than all the small grants I had received to date, including the paltry advance from Random House five years earlier. This time I chose the island of Grenada, which was even farther down the archipelago than Barbados. At a scant 133 square miles, it was also smaller than the island that was so special to me. However, while

Barbados, over time, had been pretty much reduced to a single, flat, undifferentiated field of sugarcane, Grenada was a small but gloriously variegated volcanic beauty of cratered mountains, shapely green hills, waterfalls, rivers, rainforests and valleys replete with every kind of tropical tree, foliage and vegetation imaginable. Watercress that could cost a small fortune in New York grew freely along the country roads in Grenada. As for the air: It was redolent of the nutmeg, cinnamon, cloves and other spices that were the island's economic mainstay, along with the inescapable sugarcane.

Almost fifty years have passed, yet I still vividly remember driving along a valley road in upcountry Grenada where the tall stands of bamboo on either side of our car met overhead to form an endless green-and-gold triumphal arch.

Grenada. It suggested the Eden the world had once been.

Given the substantial money in my purse this time, settling into "Eden" was on a much grander scale than before. Instead of being a mere boarder, as in Barbados, I rented a house of my own, a completely furnished old-style Creole country house, with large airy rooms, tall jalousied windows and a spacious veranda overlooking a garden that, in turn, bordered the main road that led to Grenada's capital of St. George's a few miles distant.

To staff the place and spread the wealth, I hired a housekeeper and a cook, as well as a cook's helper to do the daily marketing in town: everything from soup to nuts purchased fresh every day. A Mrs. Bishop came to do the laundry three times a week. There was also Mrs. Bishop's husband, a carpenter who couldn't find steady work. I hired him as a combination handyman, yardman and gardener.

After a number of interviews, I also found a suitable nanny for my son. She was a pleasant and capable older woman named Mrs. Charles. Better yet, Mrs. Charles had a grandson my son's age. A playmate. The book-party baby was three years old by then and had been traveling around the islands with me practically since his birth. Toddler by one hand, Royal portable by the other, and the Delancey Street suitcases in tow, I kept returning to the West Indies as simply the best and cheapest place to get the writing done.

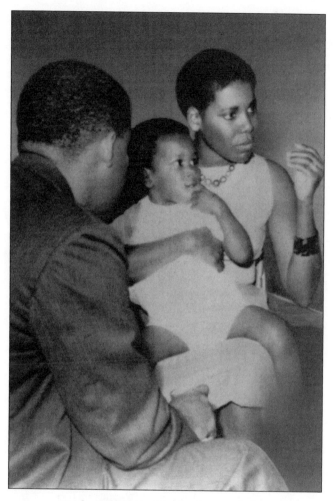

Paule with Evan, "the book party baby"

Also, before the inevitable divorce, my husband occasionally came to visit us in the West Indies. He was not an island person, however, a reaction perhaps to growing up in clannish Bajan Brooklyn. A sociology major in college, he had long been at work on a seemingly interminable doctorate whose focus was the ever-increasing youth gangs in New York with whom he had worked. His city, New York, was his great love.

Settling into Grenada would not have gone as smoothly if not for a friend I made shortly after arriving. Odessa Gittens was her name—or Miss 'Dessa, as she was called. A transplanted Bajan in her fifties and a classic civil service type, Miss 'Dessa had long worked as a health and social services officer in the poor, underserved little villages of upcountry Grenada. Odessa Gittens was a high-energy, take-charge, unapologetic maiden lady. Having seen my name and brief bio in the "Visitors to the Island" column in the local newspaper, where I was described as "an American writer of Barbadian parentage," she had promptly descended on me and taken over the settling in.

In a little over a month, then, thanks to her, we were installed in the house, a smooth-running daily routine had been established, and my son was clearly happy with Mrs. Charles and her grandson. Also, as a gift to myself, I created my own private workspace apart from the house by using the servant's room out back. I put Mr. Bishop, carpenter plus factotum, to work transforming the dark, cell-like room, with its one window and miserly cot, into a bright, airy, freshly painted workspace. It was my Virginia Woolf "room of one's own," to which, Woolf insisted, every woman writer is entitled.

In no time I had a functioning office, dominated by a large new desk purchased in town with Miss 'Dessa doing the bargaining for me. On the new desk sat the equally new Royal portable I had bought just before leaving the States—the latest model. The ample drawers of the desk were filled with enough writing supplies to last me the year I planned to spend in Grenada. Also, on top of the desk in plain view was my most valuable possession: the dozen and more steno pads containing the research material I had spent months amassing for the book I intended to write. What I had in mind was something of a historical novel, although not in the strict sense of that genre. It would be set in the present, the characters would be modern-day folk of various races and backgrounds, yet their lives, their situations, their relationships, their thinking and politics would reflect the past four-hundred-year history of the hemisphere and its continuing impact on them. In applying for the Guggenheim I had been required to submit a summary of the proposed novel. Receiving the grant seemed a stamp of approval for what I hoped to do. Moreover, I was determined that all of the historical references would be absolutely correct. Hence the stack of steno pads with their precious research notes.

In relatively short order everything was set for the writing to begin. Or so I thought. I had foolishly neglected to take the gods into account, especially the most cruel breed among them, those who delight in bestowing a gift such as a Guggenheim with one hand, only to snatch it back with the other.

The "snatching back" in my case took the form of a writer's block more massive than any I had ever suffered through before. In fact, the term "block" was woefully inadequate to describe the paralysis and impotence that came over me the moment I sat down at the desk each morning. I tried defining the cause. Was it the projected novel? Was I so intimidated by the scope of what I hoped to do that my mind, overwhelmed, had simply shut down? Perhaps it *was* too large and complex a subject for someone like me to attempt. I was still a novice, after all, someone with only one novel and a collection of stories to her name. . . .

Or could it be guilt at the Guggenheim largesse that had brought me to a standstill? Those checks in the thousands of dollars that regularly arrived from New York! And with no strings attached! No questions asked! No report on work-in-progress required! I took to blaming my woe on the bonanza of a grant. Perhaps money *did* kill creativity after all.

Or did the paralyzing guilt have to do with my being away again from the ongoing Struggle at home? When I left for Grenada there were plans to organize another massive campaign to help spur the voter-registration drive in the Deep South, especially in Mississippi. I should be on one of the buses heading southward; either that, or back in New York raising funds to support the campaign through the Artists for Freedom Organization and the other support groups to which I belonged.

Guilt over my absence from the Movement might well have been responsible for the present shutdown.

Not that I didn't try to break the paralysis. One strategy I employed was something I call "throw-away writing." I would churn out page after page of the story I desperately wanted to write, but in prose of such poor quality it was fit only for the wastepaper basket, which is where it ended up. Although inferior, the "throw-away writing" could at times offer up a word, a phrase, even a sentence that made for a breakthrough.

This was not to be the case this time.

Another tactic I tried came again from Mrs. Woolf's manifesto. "The female writer must be allowed to sit and stare, and for however long she chooses. . . ." The act of simply sitting and staring into space, she believed, allowed important information, direction, ideas, inspiration and whatever else is needed for the work at hand to emerge from the subconscious. Creative writing is, after all, both a conscious and an *unconscious* act, the two spheres of the mind working in concert to create the novel, the story, the poem.

I took V. W. at her word and, at times, simply sat and stared, waiting to be rescued by that deeper level of the self.

I also repeatedly sought help from the stack of steno pads containing my priceless research notes. Hours were spent poring over that wealth of material: I just might come across something there that would lift the paralysis and get the writing underway. I became addicted to leafing through the steno pads, hoping for a breakthrough.

All to no avail. I might as well have sought help from the lizard that took to visiting me soon after I moved in. Ever so often what seemed to be the same pale-green little creature, all five inches of it, came and encamped itself on the windowsill near me. It often spent the entire fruitless day with me. The tiny dewlap under its throat, used for mating or marking its territory, would hang there like a suspended teardrop. A gesture of sympathy perhaps on its part.

Come the late afternoon, I called a halt to the torture in the V.W. room—*Enough is enough!*—and, returning to the house, I would gather up my son. Together, just the two of us, we would set out for the nearby beach. This was our private time together each day. The beach, in this instance, was Grenada's magnificent Grand Anse, known to be one of the truly great beaches in the world. In the colonial scramble over the islands, France had lost Grenada to the British. Grand Anse, however, had retained its French name, as had much else on the island. Grand Anse meaning Great Bay. And it was just that, a wide, curving inlet over two miles long, graced from end to end with a flawless white sand beach that looked as if it were laid down fresh each morning. Equally flawless was the blue-green water of the bay—water so clear the golden mica on the seabed could be seen with the naked eye. Flawless, too, the great sweeping backdrop of palm trees that hid the one small hotel on Grand Anse at the time.

My son romped and splashed in the surf, built and destroyed any number of sand castles, chased every tiny sand crab he caught sight of back into its burrow, all the while chatting away with me. Along with the paradise of a beach, he helped me to recover, if only in part and if only temporarily, from the punishing, unproductive workday.

Our daily outing ended at sunset with the two of us sitting close together at the water's edge, our eyes trained on the horizon. We were awaiting the phenomenon Grenadians called "the green flash." The local folk swore that when the last bit of the sun vanished below the sea, there was a green flash, lasting less than the blink of an eye. This green flash, like a last hurrah to the day, occurred only at Grand Anse Beach, they said. However, not everyone was capable of seeing it. You had to be able to truly concentrate and to believe.

I never once saw the green flash, due perhaps to my frustration with the writing. On the other hand, my son, all of a sudden leaping to his feet, a small forefinger pointing, always swore that he did.

Mid-morning, and I was on the veranda taking a much-needed break from the torture chamber out back, when an old rattletrap lorry filled with country people went roaring by, horn blaring, in the direction of the capital, St. George's. A second lorry, equally packed, quickly followed, then a third, a fourth. It was soon a veritable convoy, each truck with an overload of barefoot country folk standing jammed together on the railed-in truck bed, their heads bared to an already sweltering sun. No one there seemed to mind the overcrowding, the hot sun or the deafening horns. In fact, the riders were adding their voices, a loud, happy mix of patois and English, to the din. Their repeated outbursts of laughter were like so many colorful banners they were waving to announce their descent into the capital.

A political rally. Thanks to Miss 'Dessa, who had given me a crash course in Grenadian politics just days after my arrival, I understood the significance of the convoy. I had learned that politics on the island were synonymous with one man, the long-standing chief minister, Eric Matthew Gairy, a man disdained, even hated, by the white planters and the small black and Creole bourgeoisie in town, while adored by the masses of poor black country folk. They were the majority who returned him to office each time he ran. Whenever there was the least threat to his power, he was known to dispatch a fleet of the rattletrap lorries to the countryside to round up his supporters from the canefields and spice plantations and bring them, en masse, into the capital, there to be treated to one of the spectacular rallies he held at various sites in town.

I didn't hesitate. Once the convoy ended, I informed the household that I, too, would be attending the rally. I had the cook prepare a sandwich for me to take, and with a kiss for my son I set off down the main road on foot, not bothering to wait for the public bus.

It eventually caught up with me halfway into St. George's.

In addition to the beach at Grand Anse, Grenada's other showpiece is its pretty little colonial capital. Built on a series of low-lying hills, St. George's is a picture-perfect collection of Old World French and English townhouses complete with the classic red-tiled roofs. Above the terraced houses stands Parliament, with the queen's standard aloft, while higher up, on a pair of separate hills, rise the capital's two cathedrals, Anglican and Catholic. To complete the perfection, St. George's also boasts a horseshoe-shaped deepwater harbor that is known to be among the finest in the Caribbean.

It's a favorite with the members of the yachting set who sail the West Indies during the winter.

According to what the bus driver had heard, the rally today was to be special and would therefore be held on the *carenage,* the local name for the long curving wharf that faithfully repeated the horseshoe outline of the harbor.

By the time I reached town, it was well past noon and the entire *carenage* was packed to overflowing with the chief minister's supporters. The only standing room to be found was on a narrow roadway above the harbor, where a small group of onlookers from town had already gathered. I joined them. Behind us the picturesque little capital seemed eerily quiet, deserted even, the gentry having retreated, perhaps behind their closed jalousies.

What followed was an endless wait in the crucifying mid-afternoon heat. Until, finally, what sounded like an awestruck hosanna welled up from those among the country people on the wharf who stood closest to the water. Alerted, the throngs behind them immediately joined in.

The object of the soaring paean was the distant figure of the chief minister, who could faintly be seen standing on the deck of a stately, white, flushed-deck sailboat that had just rounded the horseshoe curve of the harbor and was slowly approaching the *carenage*. Sails furled, powered solely by its motor, the sailboat majestically made its way toward the waiting crowd. Curiously, the chief minister was the only person on deck. Dressed in an impeccably tailored white suit that bespoke Savile Row and an equally bespoke pair of white dress shoes, he was standing on top of the cabin, his back flush against the main mast. In fact, he appeared to be somehow bound to the mast, his arms extended straight out from his side, and his face—the only thing black about him amid all the white—his face raised to the sky as if importuning Heaven.

All that was missing were the crown of thorns and the stigmata on his open palms.

The chief minister held the Christ-like pose all during the boat's slow passage toward the *carenage*. Only when it finally docked, with its bow directly facing his audience, did Eric Gairy slowly lower his outstretched arms, then his prayerful face, and, to another tumultuous outpouring from the crowd, he walked slowly over to the microphone awaiting him on deck.

The rally was underway.

From where I stood on the roadway it was almost impossible to follow the man's speech, given the roar of approval that punctuated almost every word he uttered. I nonetheless caught references to the many bills he was fighting to get passed in Parliament, bills that would improve the lot of his supporters. He repeatedly assured them that he never stopped putting pressure on "the damn planters" to do better by them, the country people, the hardworking people, his people. They and they alone, their welfare, was the reason he'd been called to politics. He also complained at great length about the obstructionism he faced every day in the House, even citing the names of his many enemies there. Each night he had to pray for God's help to prevail against them. Once again he assumed the crucifixion pose, arms wide, agonized face raised to Heaven. He also repeatedly reminded them of the upcoming general election. As always, he was depending on their votes. "Mark you' 'X' for Eric, *oui!* Mark you' 'X' for Eric!" The crowd immediately turned it into a chant that didn't seem to end. Another of his impassioned themes was full independence. "Finish with this so-called home rule! We want we own government, we own flag, we own anthem! And no more chief minister, but the Honorable Eric Matthew Gairy, *Prime Minister, if you please!*"

The roar of approval from the *carenage* was enough to uproot Parliament from its hill above the pretty town and send it crashing into the sea.

"Always a big show and a lotta big talk! Always fooling up the poor, ignorant country people. He ought be shame, *oui!*"

An angry outburst suddenly from a woman standing near me on the roadway. From her hawker's apron and headscarf I could tell she was an ordinary market woman. With a loud suck-teeth to underscore her disgust, she abruptly turned and walked away.

Several others there joined her.

I also left shortly afterward. Again, instead of waiting for the bus, I started back home on foot, even though it was almost dusk by now. I needed to walk, needed to put as much distance as possible, and as quickly as possible, between myself and the combination showman-demagogue still holding forth on the *carenage*.

The bus came along in due course. Then, two hours or more after it deposited me at the house, the convoy of lorries followed, headed back up-country. I had remained out on the veranda waiting for them. Again the horns were going full blast, desecrating the night silence that had fallen. This time, though, there was scarcely any talk and not a shred of laughter to be heard from the crowded truck beds. Something about their silence struck me with an appalling question: *Had they eaten for the day?* I at least had had the sandwich I'd brought along. But had they had anything to eat? Had the chief minister made any provision to feed his ardent supporters during the day-long rally? I had seen no evidence of such, not so much as a single "blugga" served, "blugga" being the local name for a particularly heavy, starchy variety of banana that was a staple upcountry. It couldn't be eaten raw—it was too tough—but once boiled until it was edible, it was known to stave off hunger for the better part of a day.

There should have been at least several large vats of boiled bluggas down on the *carenage* to feed the crowd. Along with free bottles of the sweet drink Fanta or Juice-C, or just plain water to slake their thirst.

Bread and circuses. This had been a circus all right, but without so much as a breadcrumb.

"He ought be shame, *oui.*"

The market woman's voice in my ear again.

In time, Eric Matthew Gairy's ever-faithful supporters gave him his wish. He eventually became prime minister of an independent Grenada. Although this was to be short-lived. He was ousted in a coup d'état that preceded the U.S. invasion of the island in 1983. Gairy, a minor figure in the unfortunately long and disheartening list of postcolonial leaders who misused, disappointed and failed their own.

In addition to Miss 'Dessa, another close friend I made while in Grenada was an English-woman named Heather Chambers, who taught literature in the secondary school in St. George's. A "maiden lady" like Miss 'Dessa, she, too, had chosen Grenada as home. In appearance, my teacher friend resembled the classic schoolmarm: tall, almost severe looking, her hair drawn back in a bun, and never a touch of makeup. Plain though she was, Heather Chambers nonetheless had the passion of a devotee when it came to the Big Drum/Nation Dance ceremony held every year on Grenada's tiny satellite island of Carriacou that was a mere two hours away on the local schooner.

Each year my schoolmarm friend joined those Carriacou people living in Grenada who faithfully returned home for the event.

My friend invited me to accompany her. The Big Drum/Nation Dance was not to be missed, she insisted, especially for a history buff like myself. Besides, we would only be gone overnight. We'd leave Grenada in the afternoon and be back the following morning. When I hesitated, reluctant to leave the work even though I was still making little or no progress, she enlisted Miss 'Dessa's help. My "take charge" Bajan friend was even more insistent that I go. The change would do me good. The sea breeze would do me good. The Big Drum/Nation Dance would do me even better. Also, she would sleep over at my place as extra supervision over the household and my son while I was gone.

"Go!"

Miss 'Dessa giving orders.

I went.

From the crowded deck of the schooner the following day, tiny Carriacou was scarcely visible, a mere peak on the huge subterranean mountain range that also included Grenada. Unlike Grenada, though, with its Garden of Eden beauty, Carriacou was bereft of the usual lush tropical vegetation. It seems that from the time it was colonized the island had been plagued by various crop diseases and blight. Entire fields of the prized tobacco, cotton and sugarcane repeatedly decimated. Eventually the planters—Dutch, French, British—had given up on Carriacou and, one after another, sailed away to try their luck elsewhere in the Caribbean.

Left stranded had been the chattel labor they had owned—the forebears of present-day Carriacou people.

The Big Drum/Nation Dance was held at various sites across the island. The one my friend attended each year took place in a small inland village my father would have immediately described as "a place forgotten behind God's back," what with its little tin-roofed chattel houses, its depleted-looking fields and the bare dusty gathering place at the center of the village where the yearly event was held.

From the many hugs my friend received from the villagers one would think she was a blood rela-

tive dutifully returning home for the annual ceremony. They welcomed me with equal enthusiasm.
*"America!? You's from Big America!? The
States!?"* they asked, and hugged me even more
warmly.

Shortly after dusk the ceremony got underway. At first, there didn't seem to be all that much
to the Big Drum/Nation Dance. The drums were
nothing more than a few hollowed-out logs with a
drumhead of goatskin. The drummers themselves
were elderly men who couldn't possibly, it
seemed, open their stiff, work-swollen hands to
beat a drum. I couldn't have been more wrong!
Over the course of the long night, their drums
held securely between their legs, and sustained by
the jars of white rum beside their chairs, the old
fellows proved capable of playing until dawn.

The men drummed and the women danced.
Only women performed the Nation Dance, and
mostly old women at that, the elders. It was not a
single dance, but rather a number of separate and
distinct dances, each signifying a different nation,
one of those represented by the people left
stranded when the planters fled. They knew, of

course, the name of the continent from which they had been taken. More important, even, they had retained the names of the "nations" to which they had belonged.

Who we is, *oui!* Where we's from in truth! Our true-true nation: Manding, Arada, Cromanti, Congo, Yoruba, Igbo, Chamba.

In remote little Carriacou, the names of those various nations had been carefully passed down through the generations.

Each time the old men drumming announced the theme of a particular "nation," the women who claimed it as theirs swept onto the dusty circle, which tonight had become sacred ground. Led by the elders long-schooled in the dance patterns, songs and manners of their "nation," the group repeatedly toured the circle—dancing. Wearing "their good clothes" and colorful headscarves—dancing. Arms held out at the elbows so that they resembled candelabra, the women worked their aged hips—dancing. They sang, hailing in patois the "nation" to which they traced their lineage while their bare feet spelled it out in a dusty calligraphy on the ground.

Ring Shout! I suddenly found myself remembering James Weldon Johnson's memoir *Along This Way*, which I had read as a teenager. (It had been on the list of books by colored writers that I had boldly demanded at my local library.) In the memoir, Johnson described a circular dance called the Ring Shout that the old folk in his segregated neighborhood of Jacksonville, Florida, performed nearly every night at their meeting hall. Moving in a tight circle or ring around the hall they would sing and dance and *shout!* for the better part of the night sometimes, often keeping him awake as a boy.

Johnson's Ring Shout and the Big Drum/ Nation Dance struck me as one and the same. Except, of course, that no drums were allowed at the Ring Shout. At that time drums in the hands of black folk were considered "weapons" for inciting rebellions. No matter. According to Johnson, the old folk created their own rhythm section by striking the floor in unison with the heels of their feet to create a sound as powerful as any drum as they sang and danced and *shouted* late into the night.

"We are a nation of dancers, musicians and poets," Olaudah, my adopted kinfolk, declared in his famous narrative.

Olaudah speaking of the things that sustained us in our wide dispersal.

It was long past midnight when the elderly dancers finally tired. They had acknowledged their nations, had repeatedly honored them in song and dance, and their strength had at last given out. With their departure the dusty circle that had become sacred ground under their feet was now simply a dance floor open to all. That included me as well as my schoolmarm friend, whom I repeatedly thanked for insisting that I attend the festival. A somewhat shameful confession, though: once out on the floor I had to be careful not to look at what my friend called dancing lest it throw me off step.

During the U.S. invasion of Grenada years later, Carriacou also found itself involved. President Reagan ordered that troops be sent to the little two-by-four atoll to rout out any Cuban communists who might be hiding there in its pitifully depleted fields.

For me, the idea for a novel I would write almost a decade later grew out of this overnight trip to what I would always think of as a time capsule of an island. I was scarcely aware of it back then. Yet the sense of a possible story had nonetheless implanted itself, was "on hold," so to speak, in the memory bank of my mind beyond consciousness.

Writing fiction: a wonderfully conscious and unconscious act.

Praisesong for the Widow would be the name of that future novel. In it, a well-heeled black American widow, an unapologetic bourgeoise, given to her yearly Caribbean cruise, recovers something of her true-true self after experiencing the Carriacou Big Drum/Nation Dance.

B ack in the V.W. room on the morning after the trip to Carriacou, I abruptly stopped before uncovering the typewriter and beginning another frustrating day of throw-away writing. Instead, I suddenly, purposefully gathered up the stack of steno pads containing my research notes. Next, I marched the pads, every last one of them, over to the house. There, in the storage closet, I respectfully deposited them in one of the expensive suitcases that, thanks to the Guggenheim, had replaced the Delanceys. Once all the pads were inside I closed and locked the lid of the suitcase. I also closed and locked the closet door. Then, back in the V. W. room, I sat down at the Royal, took several deep yoga breaths, and began writing my novel, finally understanding, fledgling that I still was, that as a fiction writer, a novelist, a storyteller, a fabulist, as it were, my responsibility first and foremost was to the story, the story above all else: the old verities of people, plot and place; a story that if honestly told and well crafted would resonate with the historical truths contained in the steno pads.

All of it would be there for those capable of reading in depth.

"Never let what really happened get in the way of the truth," a sage, somewhere, is known to have said.

That first day back in Grenada, the paralysis broken, I wrote nonstop until it was time for my standing date with my son at Grande Anse Beach.

The green flash at sunset?

Even with the siege lifted I still never managed to see it in our almost year-long stay in Grenada.

I'VE KNOWN
OCEANS:
THE ATLANTIC

An entire ocean permanently sitting shivah.

F ESTAC '77 was the unofficial name of the Second World Festival of Black and African Arts held in Lagos, Nigeria, in 1977. FESTAC '77 was also for me the second major plum of an all-expense-paid overseas cultural conference to come my way since the State Department tour of Europe with Mr. Hughes well over a decade earlier. This particular plum was an almost month-long festival of the arts lavishly underwritten by the Nigerian government. Its purpose was to celebrate the ending of colonialism by bringing together artists, writers and scholars from the entire continent, Cairo to Cape Town, as well as those from the far-flung African Diaspora—Brazil to Brooklyn, as it were.

It was to be nearly four weeks of performances, recitals, readings, exhibits, concerts, colloquiums, forums and the like; nearly four weeks, moreover, of meeting, conversing and interacting with fellow artists in a spirit of confraternity.

Not that FESTAC '77 didn't have its critics, the harshest being the citizenry of Lagos, the oppressively hot and humid, grossly overpopulated Nigerian capital in the Gulf of Guinea. The local folk complained bitterly about "the millions upon millions" of naira (the Nigerian dollar) being spent by the government just so that it could, as they put it, "play the high muck-a-muck" in Africa and the world; also, so that it could surpass the first and highly successful black arts festival that had been held in Dakar, Senegal, a decade earlier. (Mr. Hughes had been the official American representative to the Dakar event. The State Department had even sent him on an extensive tour of Africa when the festival ended—this, just a year before my elder friend and mentor died in 1967.)

The people of Lagos also decried the brand new National Theatre that had been built specifically for FESTAC '77. A huge, dun-gray, windowless mausoleum of a building, it was an exact copy of a theater their president had admired while on a visit to Eastern Europe. The populace was even more outraged at the rumored amount of *dash* (read: bribes) involved in the large housing complex that had been built to accommodate the thousands of visitors. The European company that finally won the contract had been forced to *dash* so liberally, it was said, that to realize a profit, the work had been shoddily done using inferior materials. Proof was the faulty plumbing and portions of the brand-new ceilings that collapsed in some of the rooms.

Dash! The modus operandi for doing business in Nigeria.

Public criticism continued unabated up to the opening day of FESTAC. Then—and apparently to no one's surprise—what looked to be the entire population of Lagos proudly turned out for the inaugural ceremony in the city's National Stadium. Inside the huge stadium, the stands were packed hours before the event was due to begin. Outside, another multitude stood angrily demanding to be admitted although there were no tickets left, the stadium of a hundred thousand completely filled. Not to be deterred, any number of daredevil young men attempted to scale the stadium's high walls. A few of them actually succeeded, only to encounter the wrath of the ticketholders in the stands as they came crashing down in their midst. Some of the men in the audience flung the gate-crashers tier by tier down the stands until they landed on the playing field. A number were seriously injured. Two, in fact, later died, according to the newspaper the following day.

An inauspicious beginning to FESTAC '77.

The opening ceremony was modeled on the Olympic Games grand parade, with each country clearly determined to outshine all the others both in pageantry and patriotic zeal. The hours-long procession was an endless display of national flags, national dress, along with outsized photographs of the national leaders (Nyerere of Tanzania, Kaunda of Zambia, Kenyatta of Kenya and the other presidents at the time) emblazoned on huge banners held aloft, as well as on the marchers' matching outfits. Each country's troupe of drummers, dancers and musicians was accompanied by a large corps of singers repeating the national anthem nonstop, all the while waving mini versions of the national flag—a veritable blizzard of the little flags—up at the stands.

The Egyptians stole the early phase of the show hands down. Not only were they among the largest delegations present, their parade was indisputably the most spectacular. Ushering their sizable troupe into the stadium was no less than a half-dozen beautifully caparisoned, fancy-stepping, white Arabian show horses—with, seated high on each of their backs, a Sahara-brown beauty. The women riders were as sumptuously costumed as their mounts in great billowing Scheherazade trousers, tunics and sheer flowing scarves. Their arms and ears bejeweled. The glint of jewels as well in their elaborately dressed hair. Kohl rimmed their eyes, adding to their drama.

Each rider was a Cleopatra look-alike holding aloft an outsized red, white and black Egyptian flag.

The crowd wildly cheered them.

Given the alphabetical order of the march, our delegation of perhaps eighty or more was positioned near the end of the massive lineup. Ours was a hot and endless wait in the holding area under the stadium. Uganda came just before us. Only after its name was finally announced and its large delegation left the holding area and were well into its march around the field was it finally our turn, the U. S. of A, us, "ussuns," Aunt Hagar's children. Unlike the other parades, ours was totally lacking in pageantry: no matching clothing or costumes, no established marching order, no well-rehearsed troupe of entertainers, no horses of any kind, no little handheld Stars 'n' Stripes to wave to the crowd and certainly no banners emblazoned with Gerald Ford's image.

Truth is, we were totally unprepared for an Olympics-style display. Not only did most in our delegation come from widely different parts of the States, many had arrived in Lagos only a day or two before the opening ceremony. There had been no time to organize even a halfway decent parade, especially one that would have satisfied the differing politics among us—these ranging from the revolutionary Black Nationalists to the moderate NAACP types and every ideology in between. Thus our parade, such as it was, turned out to be a make-do affair that reflected our divisions. One large group went charging onto the field, fists pumping in the Black Power salute, while singing, oddly, a jazzed-up, belligerent-sounding version of the old "Amen" gospel hymn.

My son, whom I had brought on the trip, was among this group. The book-party baby was all of seventeen by now, already well on his way to independent-thinking young manhood. Indeed, this would be one of our last trips together. So off he went, his raised fist like a piston in the air, his increasingly deepening voice revolutionizing the old "Amen" hymn along with the others.

Another large but more orderly group within our contingent tried drowning them out by repeatedly singing the Negro National Anthem "Lift Every Voice and Sing"—the verses they knew by heart, that is. For my part, I found myself marching with an equally large but undefined group that seemed to serve as a buffer or neutral zone between the other two.

My People. My People. Unprepared. Unrehearsed. Improvised. Disorganized.

The crowd nonetheless loved us.

From the moment the name "the United States of America" issued from the loudspeakers situated around the stadium and Aunt Hagar's offspring appeared at the entrance to the field, the stadium of a hundred thousand strong rose in a single body to roar its welcome.

The welcome continued throughout our straggly march around the huge field. Contained in the nonstop applause was pure *Omowale* joy—*Omowale* meaning, in the Yoruba language, *"The child has returned."* Their joy at our return, at our presence among them, was a hosanna heard across the length and breadth of Lagos. There was also a large, discernible measure of pride that "the displaced child" had returned representing the wealthiest and most powerful "high muck-a-muck" nation in the world. There was admiration at how the *Omowalies*, often mistreated in what was now their home, continued to agitate for their full rights as citizens: the sit-ins, the jail-ins, the marches, rallies, protests, boycotts, demonstrations, the court battles, and the leaders, heroes and foot soldiers alike who had been sacrificed in the cause.

A praise song to them all.

Indeed, the outsized, nonstop welcome was like a long traditional West African praise song that was being composed on the spot in our honor. Its excessive length was also partly driven, I sensed, by a large measure of guilt and sorrow. *As well it should be!* After all, there was the old shameful footnote of history between us: between the *Omowalies* marching in disarray around the stadium and the hundred thousand in the stands applauding us nonstop. Because hadn't their forebears been complicit, some of them, in the nefarious trade that had reduced ours—the forebears of the present day *Omowalies*—to mere articles of trade, commodities, merchandise, goods, cargo, *chattel cargo!* to be bought and sold and whipped and worked for free! And hadn't that commerce, continuing for five centuries, left us, their descendants, today's *Omowalies,* feeling at times like permanent Displaced Persons?

I know I felt that way at times. Guilt. Shame. Sorrow. They, too—if I was hearing correctly— underscored the extravagant welcome being accorded us.

All's forgiven. I said this privately, silently to an elderly woman I spotted in a front-row seat in the stands. Far too old to be on her feet applauding, she sat quietly looking on, a matriarch, an elder surrounded by the members of her family who were wildly hailing the *Omowalies* in her stead. Ancient as she was she had nevertheless dressed to the nines for the occasion. Yards of colorful, gold-threaded cloth draped her bent, dry form in an elaborate, dressed-up version of the traditional Nigerian long wrapper and blouse. An artfully arranged headscarf or *gelee,* the same palette of colors as her dress, crowned her head. As for the black, deeply lined face under the *gelee,* it appeared to be at once ancient and ageless, altogether immune to time. She could well have been alive, still only a young girl, when the first Portuguese caravel sailed into the Gulf of Guinea circa AD 1300 and the buying and selling that would continue for five hundred years began! If so, she *had* to have witnessed the collusion of her own.

Were those tears on the timeless face under the gold-threaded *gelee*? Or simply perspiration, rivulets of perspiration, given the steam-bath heat and humidity of Lagos?

I took them to be tears.

All's forgiven.

Over the next three to four weeks of FESTAC, amid the endless round of cultural events, there were many other instances of reconciliation, of forgiveness. Members of our delegation were constantly claimed, reclaimed and embraced, including even those among us who were far more white than black in appearance. Our African colleagues seemed desperate to make amends for the past. We often found ourselves the object of heated debates among them as to our possible lineage. Singling out cheekbones, foreheads, the shape of our eyes, our heads, the size and design of our lips, the particular spread and flare to our nostrils, our jawlines, examining all this they would declare us to be variously Yoruba, Fanti, Ibo, Akan, Igbo, Fulani, Temne, Luo. . . .

At a reception following a large-scale reading in which I participated, a bearded poet from Ghana hurried over to claim that I was pure Ashanti. The fleshy knob at the end of my nose was a distinctly Ashanti feature, according to him. He was immediately challenged by a young schoolteacher from Zambia in the crowd gathered around us. According to the schoolteacher I looked exactly like an aunt of his and therefore had to be of the Bemba people. In fact, the resemblance was so strong, he said, he considered me to be his aunt's American twin. Indeed, whenever I encountered the young schoolteacher afterward, he would tender me a respectful little bow reserved for an elder. The same one, I'm sure, he accorded his aunt, "my Bemba twin," in Zambia.

To be claimed by so many! To possess a face that was generic apparently to the entire continent below the Sahara!

FESTAC '77 ended with a palm-wine gala on the roof terrace of the ugly, showpiece National Theatre. I spent most of the party reassuring my friends among the African writers that this would not be my sole visit to the continent. I had to keep promising them that my return was a foregone conclusion as far as I was concerned.

After all, my life, as I saw it, was a thing divided in three: There was Brooklyn, U.S.A., and specifically the tight, little, ingrown immigrant world of Bajan Brooklyn that I had fled. Then, once I started writing, the Caribbean and its conga line of islands had been home off and on for any number of years. While all the time, lying in wait across the Atlantic, in a direct line almost with tiny wallflower Barbados, had been the Gulf of Guinea and the colossus of ancestral Africa, the greater portion of my tripartite self that I had yet to discover, yet to know.

Of course I would be back! In fact, I could have confided to my friends on the roof terrace that while packing my suitcases earlier in the day I had already started thinking of how to underwrite my return. Africa, it was clear, would call for a higher order of grant than the Guggenheim that had supported me so handsomely in Grenada. Also, the Guggenheim had been only for a year. The long, leisurely sojourn south of the Sahara I had in mind would require one of the truly heavyweight grants, a Rockefeller or Ford Foundation. Or the kind of State Department–sponsored cultural tours that had sent Mr. Hughes repeatedly around the world. Or a Fulbright! A generous, unlimited Fulbright that would allow me to remain on the Mother Continent writing, doing research, traveling—and with no questions asked, no strings attached.

Dare I hope?

I raised my glass of palm wine to Lady Luck. Happily, she didn't disappoint me. Her help wasn't in the form of a heavyweight grant. (That would come a decade later with the MacArthur Fellowship.) Instead, three years after FESTAC the Kenyan government invited a group of black American artists and writers, including yours truly, to visit the country, all expenses paid. On my own, I included a side trip to Uganda, which, unfortunately, proved to be an unwise choice at the time. I also tried but failed to enter Tanzania as well as Zambia, home of my Bemba twin.

At present, I'm in the throes of writing about that limited and frustrating East African experience. Then it'll be back to my primary love: the novel, the short story.